Oppressed in the Land?

PRINCETON SERIES OF MIDDLE EASTERN SOURCES IN TRANSLATION

General Editor, M. Şükrü Hanioğlu

Oppressed in the Land?

Fatwās on Muslims Living under Non-Muslim Rule from the Middle Ages to the Present

ALAN VERSKIN

Markus Wiener Publishers
Princeton

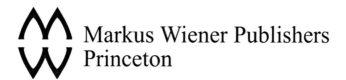

Cover illustration: Portulan de la mer Méditerranée by ʿAlī b. Aḥmad b. Muḥammad al-Sharqī. Bibliothèque nationale de France, Department of Manuscripts, Arabe 2278, f. 2v.

For information, write to: Markus Wiener Publishers
231 Nassau Street, Princeton, NJ 08542
www.markuswiener.com

Library of Congress Cataloging-in-Publication Data
Verskin, Alan
Oppressed in the land? : fatwas on Muslims living under non-Muslim rule from the Middle Ages to the present / Alan Verskin.
p. cm. — (Princeton series of Middle Eastern sources in translation)
Includes bibliographical references.
ISBN 978-1-55876-571-9 (hardcover : alk. paper)
ISBN 978-1-55876-572-6 (pbk. : alk. paper)
1. Fatwas. 2. Muslims—Non-Muslim countries. 3. Muslims—Legal status, laws, etc. I. Title.
KBP491.V47 2013
340.5'9—dc23
2012036267

Markus Wiener Publishers books are printed in the United States of America on acid-free paper and meet the guidelines for permanence and durability of the Committee on Production Guidelines for Book Longevity of the Council on Library Resources.

For My Father

CONTENTS

Acknowledgments ix

Introduction 1

Fatwās and Muftīs 3
Muslims under Non-Muslim Rule 6
Notes on These Translations 16

1. The End of Muslim Spain 19

Al-Wansharīsī on the Leader of the Muslims of Christian Marbella 21
Al-Ramlī on the Muslims of Christian Spain 31

2. Rulers Who Falsely Claim to Be Muslims 35

Ibn Taymiyya on the Town of Mārdīn under the Mongols 35
ʿUthmān Ibn Fūdī and Hausaland 39
Interpretations of Ibn Fūdī in the Age of British Imperialism in Hausaland 47

3. India 51

Fatwās in Favor of British Rule 58
Karamat ʿAli: British India Is the Abode of Islam 63
Sayyid Ahmad Khan: On the Ambiguous Status of India 80
The 1920 Hijrat to Afghanistan 83
The End of Calls for Migration from India 88

4. The French in North Africa 91

Muḥammad b. Aḥmad ʿIllaysh on the Muslims of French Algeria 95

Fatwās for the French 98
Fatwās for the French in Mauritania 104

5. The Birth of Minority Jurisprudence
(*Fiqh al-aqalliyyāt*) 113
Rashīd Riḍā: Must Muslims Leave
Austro-Hungarian Bosnia? 117

6. Minority Jurisprudence (*Fiqh al-aqalliyyāt*)
in the Twentieth Century 129
Against Minority Jurisprudence –
The Views of Saʿīd Ramaḍān al-Būṭī 145

Appendix: Israel/Palestine 149

*Suggestions for Further Reading in English
on Muslims under Non-Muslim Rule* 157

ACKNOWLEDGMENTS

This book has been many years in the making. I first became interested in the issue of Muslims living under non-Muslim rule while writing a dissertation at Princeton University on Islamic legal responses to the Spanish Reconquista and the reception of these responses during the French colonization of the nineteenth-century Maghrib. During this period, I greatly benefited from discussions on the topic with my dissertation advisor, Michael Cook, and my dissertation committee, Muhammad Qasim Zaman, Avraham Udovitch, and Lawrence Rosen.

In response to the questions of students and colleagues, I began to think beyond Spain and the Maghrib while teaching Islamic studies in the International Studies Department of Macalester College. This interest developed further when I taught the following year in another international environment, the Department of Middle Eastern, South Asian and African Studies at Columbia University. I would like to thank my colleagues and students at both Macalester and Columbia for challenging me to expand the focus of my scholarship, and to think seriously about what it means to study a "world religion."

Many of my colleagues have contributed to my thinking on this topic: Wael Hallaq, Katharina Ivanyi, Brinkley Messick, Timothy Mitchell, David Moore, Khaldoun Samman, and Franz Bibfeldt. I would like to thank two colleagues in particular: Najam Haider, who first gave me the idea that this book would be a good one to write, and Brett Wilson who warmly welcomed me to the Midwest and to my first academic job. I am also indebted to my publisher, Markus Wiener, for his mentorship and friendship since I first met him in Princeton when I was a graduate student.

The research for this book was funded in part by a New Faculty Fellowship from the American Council of Learned Societies and Columbia University.

I would like to thank my wife, Sara, who has not only encouraged me but also helped me at every stage and in every way with this book—its conceptualization, the translations, and the editing. I owe a debt of gratitude to my parents-in-law who, in addition to producing my wife, also read through this entire manuscript. My children, Maya, Hannah, and Daniel, are also to be thanked for their toleration of my absences and of my mounds of books and papers in our living room, which they have chosen to variously avoid or incorporate into their games.

This book is dedicated to my father, Milton Verskin, who started me on my intellectual journey and has accompanied me on it all the way.

Introduction

Do "good Muslims" have to live in a country governed by Muslims? If they do, what are they obliged to do if they find themselves under non-Muslim rule? If they do not, what kinds of conditions need to exist in a non-Islamic country in order for Muslims to live there, how does living in such a country affect religious practice, and how should religious identity affect political loyalty?

Many events in world history have prompted Muslims to ask themselves these questions. Sometimes these questions arose as the result of conquests of Muslim lands. In the medieval period, such conquests included those by Christians of Muslim territories in Spain, Portugal, and southern Italy and those by the Mongols (who originally were non-Muslim, but who eventually converted to Islam) of large swaths of the Middle East. Questions of life under non-Muslim rule also arose during the medieval period as a result of the extensive communities of Muslim traders who lived beyond the Islamic world. For example, Muslim traders lived among Hindus and Buddhists along the Silk Road and in Southeast Asia, and among animists in sub-Saharan Africa. The questions developed in a slightly different form in the case of rulers who self-identified as Muslim, but whose Muslim identity was called into question on account of their allegedly un-Islamic practices. In the premodern period, this often occurred in areas of Africa where a process of gradual Islamization did not completely eliminate pre-Islamic beliefs and practices. Later, in the age of European imperialism and expansion, Muslims across the world became subjects of Austro-Hungarian, British, Dutch, French, Russian, and other European powers. In the twentieth century, the issue again came to prominence when Muslims lost territorial control to the Jewish state of Israel. Finally, mostly in the latter half of the twentieth century, millions of Muslims have come to live in non-Muslim countries not through conquest but through immigration, and largely by choice. The issue of life under non-Muslim rule has thus garnered considerable attention over the centuries from an international set of scholars. The subject should therefore be of interest not only to students of Islamic law but also to those interested in colonialism, diaspora studies, interfaith relations, and world history.

Who decides what Islam does and does not permit a Muslim to do? Contemporary Muslims answer that question in many different ways. Historically, however, the interpretation of what Islam mandates, permits, discourages, and prohibits has usually been understood as the domain of Islamic jurisprudence (*fiqh*). What follows is a very brief overview of a subject to which jurists have devoted thousands of volumes over the centuries.[1] Islamic jurisprudence is written by jurists, but it is not understood as a law that is made by jurists. Rather, Islamic jurisprudence is a process by which jurists come to understand the content of the Law (*Sharīʿa*) that God has ordained. The jurists understand there to be two primary sources from which the *Sharīʿa* can be discovered: the Qurʾān (which Muslims believe consists of verses revealed by God to the Prophet Muḥammad on various occasions over a period of many years) and the *sunna*, the statements and behavior of the Prophet, who is understood to be morally exemplary. The example set by the Prophet is passed down in the *ḥadīth* (traditions). Each *ḥadīth* tells a story about what the Prophet or his companions said or did, together with a list of who learned the tradition from whom.

The *Sharīʿa* can also be discovered from other sources, among which is the consensus (*ijmāʿ*) of the jurists. One scholar gives the following definition of this term: "Consensus . . . means that 'society' in some form—all Muslims, or the scholars, or a selection of them—through their agreement establish that specific legal rules are part of God's law, the *Sharīʿa*. Society confirms the law that God gave society."[2] Why this should be the case, how a consensus

1. For an overview of the key elements of Islamic jurisprudence, see Wael Hallaq, *A History of Islamic Legal Theories: An Introduction to Sunnī Uṣūl al-Fiqh* (Cambridge: Cambridge University Press, 1999), and Bernard Weiss, *The Spirit of Islamic Law* (Athens: University of Georgia Press, 1998).

2. Knut Vikør, *Between God and the Sultan: A History of Islamic Law* (Oxford: Oxford University Press, 2005), 76.

was to be determined, and on what range of issues it could exist was, however, extensively debated by the jurists. The fourth means of determining the *Sharīʿa* is *ijtihād*, or independent judicial reasoning. *Ijtihād* allows the greatest scope for jurists to make their own law, and it has therefore been the subject of much debate. There have been numerous attempts to restrict its application, because the legislative power that it gives to individual jurists can potentially destabilize the legal system. *Ijtihād* can occur in many forms. At its simplest, it merely involves finding relevant passages in the Qurʾān, *ḥadīth*, and legal works and deducing from them what the law is for cases that have not been explicitly dealt with. Some jurists also allowed for *ijtihād* to be made on the basis of considering what laws would be necessary for communal welfare.[3] Activities that are central to communal welfare were generally defined as those that promote the maintenance of the five general aims of the law: the preservation of religion (*dīn*), life, reason, property, and lineage.[4] Determining whether a ruling is a legitimate reflection of the divinely ordained *Sharīʿa* is thus multifaceted, and it is easy to see how jurists could come to vastly different conclusions as a result of their deliberations.

Fatwās and Muftīs

The jurists wrote in a variety of genres. They wrote, for example, legal manuals, judgments, and commentaries on the Qurʾān's legal passages. The genre from which most of the works in this anthology are taken, however, is that of the *fatwā* (responsum). A fatwā is an answer to a question about how the law applies to a given situation. Unlike the laws of a legal manual, a fatwā is not an abstract formulation of the law but rather a statement about how the heavenly ideal of the law should apply in practice. A jurist who answers legal questions is called a *muftī*. The typical question (*istiftā*) and

3. Jurists use different terms to designate this concept, including *maṣlaḥa*, *istiṣlāḥ*, and *istiḥṣān*.

4. For a general outline of these principles, see Weiss, *Spirit of Islamic Law*, 170.

answer include several components. The question usually begins with an invocation of God, followed by a statement of the concern at hand, followed by a request that the *muftī* use his knowledge of Islamic law to address it. Often this request ends with the pious hope that the *muftī* will be rewarded by God for his response.

The components of a fatwā vary considerably, but they usually involve the following. After invoking God, the *muftī* attempts to pinpoint which legal categories, cases, and terminology are applicable to the situation at hand. This sometimes involves explaining which legal categories are *not* applicable, and why it is a mistake to think that they pertain to the situation. Sometimes the *muftī*, in so doing, will reformulate the original question, change its focus, supply new alternatives, or pose an extra set of questions in addition to the issues raised in the original question. In supplying an answer, the *muftī* will usually attempt to find support for his position in verses from the Qurʾān and/or statements from *ḥadīth*s. When citing verses, the *muftī* often chooses not simply to quote the verse alone but to quote it together with glosses, commentaries, or interpretations that have been written about it. Some of these interpretations may conflict with each other and some may even conflict with views espoused by the *muftī,* but he quotes them to indicate that his views are not the product of his own arbitrary interpretation of religious texts but rather stand in dialogue with a long line of scholars who have thought deeply on these issues. If earlier legal sources deal with the problem at hand, the *muftī* will also quote them. It is thus not uncommon for a fatwā to cite other fatwās.

For the reader new to the study of fatwās, the sheer volume of proof-texts, precedents, and authorities may seem tedious or overwhelming. However, it is precisely these foundations which lend authority and authenticity to a *muftī*'s opinion. From a glance at the sources which a *muftī* cites, the expert can get a sense of the degree of the *muftī*'s learning and of the circle of scholars to which he belongs.

It should be noted that the subject matter which fatwās can address is broad in scope. Fatwās do not deal only with the legal ramifications of interpersonal disputes but with nearly all aspects of life. They can involve such diverse questions as: What does Islam have to say about vegetarianism? Can young people of the opposite sex chat on the internet with each other? Is in-vitro fertilization Islamically acceptable? What obligations do adult children have when taking care of their elderly parents and in-laws? What should people say when visiting the sick or comforting a bereaved friend? The vast breadth of the genre has given *muftī*s considerable freedom to express themselves.

What was the audience for a fatwā? In the past, most requests for fatwās came from judges who needed a clarification of the law for a case at hand. However, beginning in the nineteenth century, questions to *muftī*s began to come in significant numbers from the laity.[5] Bearing this in mind, it is important to consider the pedagogical role of the fatwā. Generally, a request for a fatwā is made only in cases where the position of the law on a given matter is unclear. However, the clarity of the law is, of course, a matter of perspective. A person who does not have a legal education or law books at his disposal might refer a relatively clear-cut legal question to the *muftī*. It is for this reason that some have understood fatwās as a mode of popularizing the law.[6]

In Islamic law, a fatwā is regarded as nonbinding. In the contemporary period, some Muslims have interpreted this to mean that a fatwā has no force whatsoever. One scholar, in summarizing this view, says, "a *fatwa* . . . is a non-binding legal opinion, and Muslims choose which fatwa they will and will not apply to their lives. In this regard, Muslims participate in a 'free market' of religious thought."[7] However, in the classical period of Islamic jurisprudence, a fatwā was regarded as having considerably greater force than is implied by this quotation. As Wael Hallaq writes: "True,

5. Barbara Metcalf, *Islamic Revival in British India: Deoband, 1860-1900* (Oxford: Oxford University Press, 2005), 50.

6. Juan Martos Quesada, "Características del muftí en al-Andalus: contribución al estudio de una institución jurídica hispanomusulmana," *Anaquel de estudios árabes* 7 (1996), 128.

7. J. Esposito, *Who Speaks For Islam? What a Billion Muslims Really Think* (New York: Gallup Press, 2007), 54-55.

unlike the magistrate's decision, the jurisconsult [*muftī*'s] legal opinion [*fatwā*] was not binding, but his opinion, by virtue of its having emanated from a highly qualified authority, became part of, and indeed defined, the law; . . . the jurisconsults' *fatwā* is universal . . . and applicable to *all* similar cases that may arise in the future."[8] Another scholar writes, "The significance of the work of the muftis—whether private or public—rests on the high degree of authority that could be carried by their opinions, which represent the closest Islamic equivalent to the familiar Anglo-American legal mechanism of case-law precedent."[9] A fatwā was therefore not something which individuals could arbitrarily accept or reject according to their own preferences. As Norman Calder writes: "A fatwa must be followed, whether by the judge or by the petitioner, unless there is reason based in knowledge for rejecting it. Only a jurist of some ability could discover a reason, based in knowledge, for rejecting a fatwa."[10] A situation in which everyone was free to exercise their own judgment as to what the law should be on matters which could have deep spiritual, social, and political significance was to be avoided. As Jalāl al-Dīn al-Suyūṭī (d. 911/1505) remarked, "If everyone were a muftī there would be chaos."[11]

Muslims under Non-Muslim Rule

When Muslims wrote about issues pertaining to life under non-Muslim rule in the premodern period, they generally did so in fatwās, which were the traditional venue for dealing with new or unusual situations. Once some consensus on the issues had been built, a more refined version of the laws developed in fatwās could

8. Hallaq, *A History of Islamic Legal Theories*, 154.

9. Muhammad Masud, Brinkley Messick, and David Powers, "Muftis, Fatwas, and Islamic Legal Interpretation," in *Islamic Legal Interpretation: Muftīs and Their Fatwas* (Cambridge: Harvard University Press, 1996), 4.

10. Norman Calder, *Islamic Jurisprudence in the Classical Era*, ed. Colin Imber (Cambridge: Cambridge University Press, 2010), 128.

11. Quoted in E. M. Sartain, *Jalāl al-Dīn al-Suyūṭī* (Cambridge: Cambridge University Press, 1975), 63.

be introduced into a legal manual.[12] When Muslims needed answers to new questions, they therefore turned to a *muftī*, who would give an answer tailored to their particular circumstances. The questions asked of *muftī*s about living under non-Muslim rule were many. Among them were: Can Muslims live in a society governed by non-Muslims so long as they allow them to freely practice their religion? What does it mean to practice religion freely? What if Muslims fear that a non-Islamic government's policy might change and that it might pressure them or offer them incentives to convert to another religion? If a non-Muslim official appoints religious leaders for Muslims, are those leaders legitimate? Is it better to live in a non-Islamic land if one can earn a living there, or to live in an Islamic one dependent on the charity of others? What are Muslims obliged to do if a non-Islamic govemment asks them to join the military and to fight against fellow Muslims? How should Muslims who collaborate with an "anti-Islamic" government be treated? What if a ruler claims to be Islamic, but the sincerity of this claim is doubted? Should Muslim communities leave *en masse* areas that have come under non-Muslim control, even if it means leaving those few Muslims who remain in a dangerous position? If Muslims stay in an area that has been conquered, can they apply for citizenship, join the military, join the government, and otherwise participate in activities which will end up strengthening and enriching their non-Muslim conquerors?

Over the centuries such questions have elicited a wide variety of answers, all of which involved consideration of the political experiences of the Prophet Muḥammad (d. 9/632). Muḥammad's life is traditionally divided into two phases. A first, largely apolitical, phase coincided with his early life in pagan Mecca. A second phase, beginning with his migration (*hijra*) to Medina (0 H./622 A.D.), is one in which he assumed a role of political leadership. Having been invited to settle in Medina in a desperate bid to halt the destructive blood feuding of its tribes, he responded by replac-

12. Wael Hallaq, "From *Fatwā*s to *Furū'*: Growth and Change in Islamic Substantive Law," *Islamic Law and Society* 1 (1994), 29-65.

ing the failed political order with a new one. He introduced a constitution that mandated that blood ties be replaced by ties of religion. Because, according to the constitution, all members of Medina constituted a single group of "kin" by virtue of their new shared faith, the basis of the blood feud would be undermined. He also instituted laws regulating the collection of alms, inheritance, and family matters. An important part of Muḥammad's early mission was, therefore, the pursuit of social justice through political means. Muḥammad's course of action indicates that he believed that Islam could and should have a positive impact on the social order. He did not believe that it should be relegated to a domain of personal ritual that could not respond to the pressing political problems of the day. Because life under non-Muslim rule meant that Muslims would not be able to actualize these political visions of social justice, the jurists had to determine how this predicament could be reconciled with the ideals exemplified by Muḥammad in Medina. Was it permissible for Muslims to limit themselves to the practice of Islamic ritual and effectively ignore broader sociopolitical issues?

The case against indifference to Muḥammad's political project is forcefully made in the Qur'ān, where those who chose not to participate in it, by neglecting to migrate to the Islamic polity, are negatively stigmatized. Consider, for example, the following passage:

> Those who believed and left their homes and strove with their wealth and lives in God's cause, and those who took them in and helped them: these are allies of one another. And those who believed but did not leave their homes, you have no duty to protect them until they leave their homes. But if they seek help from you in a religious matter, then it is your duty to help them, except against a people between whom and you there is a treaty. . . . Those who believed and left their homes and strove for God's cause, and those who took them in and helped them—these, in truth, are the believers.[13]

13. Qur'ān 8: 72-74. Translations of the Qur'ān are adapted from those of M. Pickthall.

This passage contrasts three groups, all of whom are considered to be Muslims. A common traditional understanding of the passage[14] identifies the first group as consisting of Meccan Muslims who migrated from their homes to Medina. It identifies the second group as consisting of Meccan Muslims who chose to remain in Mecca under the rule of non-Muslims. It identifies the third group as consisting of the Medinan Muslims who took in the Meccan migrants. An important assumption underlying this interpretation is that the religious bond between the Meccan migrants and their Medinan helpers trumps the blood ties between the two Meccan groups. It is the Meccan migrants and their Medinan helpers who, "in truth, are the believers." As for the Meccan Muslims who remained in Mecca, their commitment to faith is clearly acknowledged as a positive act, but, because it is not accompanied by any political commitment, it is not enough to give them the privileges of full membership in the Muslim community. Because they have not offered their political assistance to the Muslim community, that community is not under an obligation to help them.

As the above passage implies, migrating to the Muslim community was an important part of what it meant to be a Muslim during the early Islamic period.[15] The Qur'ān emphasizes that migration is obligatory from lands in which people are forced to commit wrongdoing. Those who do not migrate under such circumstances are condemned to hell. There they will be held accountable even for the wrongdoing they committed under duress because they could have avoided that duress through migration. There are also Qur'ānic verses which do not mention the issue of committing wrongdoing under duress, but which simply describe migration as an act of commitment to the community of believers.[16] Believers who do not perform migration are not condemned to hell; how-

---

14. See, for example, J. Burton (ed.), "*Abū 'Ubaid al-Qāsim b. Sallām's K. al-nāsikh wa-l-mansūkh" (Ms. Istanbul, Topkapi, Ahmet III A 143)* (Cambridge: E. J. W. Gibb Memorial Trust, 1987), 143 ff.

15. Patricia Crone, "The First-Century Concept of *Hiğra*," *Arabica* 61 (1994), 352 - 387.

16. See, for example, Qur'ān 8: 72: *wa-jāhadū bi-amwālihim wa-anfusihim fī sabīl allāhi*. Cf. Qur'ān 8: 75, 9: 19-20, and 16: 110.

ever, the believing community has "no duty of alliance" towards them.[17] Because they have not offered their political assistance to the Muslim community, that community is not under an obligation to help them. True believers in this early period are thus those who live in communities that are governed by Muslims.

Later jurists distilled these descriptions of the lives of the early believers drawn from the Qur'ān and the *ḥadīth* into the judicial categories of the "abode of Islam" and the "abode of war." One scholar explains these categories thus: "Muslims lived in *dār al-Islām* [the abode of Islam]. . . . This was the world in which Islamic law held sway and in which there were rights and duties, human warmth, peace, and brotherhood. Infidels lived in *dār al-kufr*, the abode of unbelief, also known as *dār al-ḥarb*,[18] the abode of war. . . . The relationship between them was deemed to be one of war, whether latent or actively pursued."[19] One might think that this stark contrast would have entirely prohibited Muslims from living in non-Muslim territory or from having anything to do with its residents. However, the contrast was nuanced by several factors. Individual non-Muslims from the abode of war could receive safe-conducts (*amān*), similar to a modern day travel visa, which would allow them to temporarily reside in safety in the abode of Islam. A holder of this safe-conduct was known as a *musta'min*. More significantly, Islamic law recognized a category between the abode of Islam and the abode of war that could be created by way of a treaty which curtailed hostilities. Once a treaty was ratified, the abode of war ceased to be called thus and became the abode of treaty (*dār al-ʿahd*). The jurists, however, recommended that such treaties be made only as a temporary measure.

Some jurists also mitigated the severity of the contrast between the abode of Islam and the abode of war by changing the definition of the abode of Islam to mean not a land governed by a Muslim ruler, but one in which Muslims could freely observe Islam,

17. Qur'ān 8: 72.

18. Although these terms are largely synonymous in the classical period, some later jurists, as discussed in this volume, draw distinctions between them.

19. Patricia Crone, *God's Rule: Government and Islam* (New York: Columbia University Press, 2004), 359.

regardless of the religion of the ruler. One of the earliest jurists to take this position was al-Māwardī (d. 450/1058). He said that, provided that a Muslim was able to publicly practice Islam in a territory ruled by non-Muslims, that territory was considered a part of the abode of Islam.[20] This categorization could potentially allow for non-Muslim lands to receive the status of "abode of Islam" even if they did not have a Muslim government. Many subsequent jurists agreed with al-Māwardī's opinion. However, as one scholar has noted, "there is no consensus among jurists with regard to the level of freedom necessary for Muslims in non-Muslim territory."[21] Some contend that the minimum level of freedom involves Muslims being free to conduct their prayers in public. Others believe that the minimum level must involve full freedom in the area of family law or even full communal autonomy and exemption from non-Islamic laws.[22]

A major barrier to living under non-Muslim rule was the belief that it would violate the hierarchy which, already in the Qurʾān, is set between Islam and other religions. Islam is sent by God in order "to prevail over all religion" (Qurʾān 48: 28).[23] This was understood to mean that Islam and Muslims should enjoy a privileged place in society, and that those who chose not to embrace the religion should have the opposite status.[24] This sentiment is encapsulated in a frequently cited *ḥadīth*, "Islam is exalted and nothing is exalted above it."[25] This principle of order is represented in the hierarchical structure of the Islamic polity. Non-Muslims who were "people of the book," defined by the Qurʾān as Christians (*naṣāra*), Jews (*al-yahūd*, *Banū Isrāʾīl*), and Sabians (*ṣābiʾūn*), but sometimes also extended to other communities, were entitled to continue to practice their religion in exchange for accepting a set of legal disabili-

20. Khaled Abou El Fadl, "Islamic Law and Muslim Minorities: The Juristic Discourse on Muslim Minorities from the Second/Eighth to the Eleventh/Seventeenth Centuries," *Islamic Law and Society* 1 (1994), 150.

21. Abou El Fadl, "Islamic Law and Muslim Minorities," 159.

22. Ibid.

23. Cf. Qurʾān 9: 33 and 61: 9.

24. Qurʾān 2: 61, 3: 112, and 9: 29.

25. *Ṣaḥīḥ al-Bukhārī* (Cairo: Dār al-Muḥaddithīn, 2007), no. 1288: "al-Islām yaʿlū wa-lā yuʿlā." This *ḥadīth* is discussed in Y. Friedman, *Tolerance and Coercion in Islam: Interfaith Relations in the Muslim Tradition* (Cambridge: Cambridge University Press, 2003), 35 ff.

ties outlined in a pact (*dhimma*), the provisions of which gave tangible representation to the Islamic hierarchy of religions. The pact included political provisions, such as a special poll-tax (*jizya*) levied on male subjects (*dhimmīs*) and promises that the non-Muslim population would aid the Muslims rather than their enemies. The pact contained religious provisions limiting the spread of non-Muslim religions by forbidding the construction of houses of worship and conversion to religions other than Islam. Lastly, it included rules to clearly delineate Muslim and non-Muslim populations and to demonstrate the superiority of the one over the other. For example, non-Muslims were prohibited from affecting Islamic dress and giving their children Islamic-sounding names. The houses of non-Muslims could not be built higher than those of Muslims, and they had to give up their seats to Muslims. The enforcement of the pact, which was highly dependent on the disposition of the political ruler, varied considerably throughout the Islamic world. However, regardless of its degree of enforcement, it remained a juristic ideal.[26] To accept an inversion of this ideal by imposing on Muslims a duty of obedience to a non-Muslim ruler was naturally seen by many jurists as a perversion of the divinely ordained order. Jurists differed regarding the weight that they gave this hierarchy in their decisions about Muslims living under non-Muslim rule, but it was nonetheless widely referenced.

The jurists also worried that Muslim life in non-Muslim society would lead to Muslims becoming assimilated into the non-Muslim society. For example, jurists commented on how Muslims living under Christian rule in medieval Spain came to imitate Christians by participating in Christian ceremonies and festivals, drinking their wine, eating forbidden food, speaking their language, losing their knowledge of Arabic, and wearing their style of clothing.[27]

---

26. Mark R. Cohen, "What Was the Pact of 'Umar? A Literary-Historical Study," *JSAI* 23 (1999), 100–157, and Milka Levy-Rubin, *Non-Muslims in the Early Islamic Empire: From Surrender to Coexistence* (New York: Cambridge University Press, 2011).

27. Fernando de la Granja, "Fiestas cristianas en al-Andalus," *al-Andalus* 35 (1970), 119-42; Gerard Wiegers, "Language and Identity: Pluralism and the Use of Non-Arabic Languages in the Muslim West," in *Pluralism and Identity: Studies in Ritual Behaviour*, ed. Jan Platvoet et al. (Leiden: Brill, 1995), 303 ff.; John Boswell, *The Royal Treasure* (New Haven, CT: Yale University Press, 1977), 381 ff.; and L. P. Harvey, *Islamic Spain, 1250 to 1500* (Chicago: University of Chicago Press, 1990), 90.

The issue of assimilation continues to be extensively discussed during the modern period in literature about Muslim minorities.

Historically, the question of whether Muslims could live under non-Muslim rule was not dealt with extensively by the jurists in the pre-modern period. The Islamic world was large and, for the most part, powerful, and it was an unusual situation for Muslims to find themselves permanently living outside of it. The question tended to be asked in times of great communal distress brought about by the loss of Muslim lands. In one of the earliest recorded responses to this issue, Muslim scholars answered a question regarding the legal consequences of the conquest of Baghdad by Mongol non-Muslims. Notably, the question was not posed by Muslims themselves, but was posed by the conqueror, who did so in order to ensure the obedience of his subjects:

> When in 656/1258 the sultan Hulāgū conquered Baghdad, he asked the religious sages for a legal opinion (*fatwā*) on the question: who is preferable, an unbelieving ruler who is righteous, or a Muslim ruler who is unjust? He convened the religious sages for this purpose in the al-Mustanṣiriyya religious school (*madrasa*). When they were faced with the text of the proposed legal opinion, they refrained from responding. . . . Among them on that occasion was the learned man Rashīd al-Dīn ʿAlī ibn Ṭaʾūs, who enjoyed a position of seniority and prestige. When he saw that they did not respond, he took the written *fatwā* and confirmed and signed it. The text said that a just unbeliever was, in fact, preferable to an unjust Muslim. The other sages then followed suit and also concurred.[28]

The scholars were clearly not pleased with the prospect of endorsing the view that an unbelieving ruler who is righteous is better than a Muslim ruler who is unjust. Such a view would serve to justify the non-Muslim conqueror and nullify the value set upon having an Islamic sociopolitical structure. Nonetheless the jurists, in the face of the enormous power of the Mongol ruler, supported the

---

28. Muḥammad b. ʿAlī Ibn al-Ṭiqṭaqa (d. 709/1309), *al-Fakhrī fī al-ādāb al-sulṭāniyya* (Paris: Bouillon, 1895), 21. Quoted in J. Sadan "'Community' and 'Extra-Community' as a Legal and Literary Problem," *IOS* 10 (1980), 114.

view as a result of painful necessity and so paved the way for allowing Muslims to live under such rulers. This pattern of behavior is typical of many subsequent encounters between Muslim scholars and non-Muslim conquerors. As we shall see, even in the modern era, European imperial powers solicited such opinions in an effort to reconcile their Muslim subjects to their rule.

More recently, however, some Muslims have seen living under non-Muslim rule not as a tragic necessity but as an opportunity to propagate Islam. Thus Yūsuf al-Qaraḍāwī, one of the leading contemporary voices on the issue of Muslims living under non-Muslim rule, says:

> There can be no questioning of the permissibility of residing in a non-Muslim country . . . if we were to forbid it . . . we would close the door to the call to Islam and its spread throughout the world. [Had this been done] . . . the Islam of old would have been restricted to the Arabian peninsula. . . . If we read history and reflect upon it properly we find that the spread of Islam into the lands that we today refer to as the Arabic and Islamic worlds occurred through the influence of individual Muslims, merchants, Sufis and others like them, who migrated from their countries to those lands in Asia and Africa and mixed with the local people, worked together with them and in turn were liked by them for their good morals and sincerity, as was their religion which had implanted these virtues in them. Thus people entered our religion en masse and individually.[29]

This kind of thinking is largely unprecedented in classical Islamic thought but has found increasing support in the contemporary period.

The reader of this anthology will discover that there is no static answer to the question of whether Muslims can live under non-Muslim rule. Over the centuries, Muslims have developed a wide variety of ways to answer this question. There are opinions that it is desirable for Muslims to live in non-Muslim lands, there are opinions that it is forbidden for Muslims to live in such lands, and

29. Yūsuf al-Qaraḍāwī, *Fī fiqh al-aqalliyyāt al-muslima* (Cairo: Dār al-Shurūq, 2001), 33. Quoted in Andrew March, *Islam and Liberal Citizenship* (Oxford: Oxford University Press, 2009), 173.

there are many opinions in between. This diversity is not a product of the modern period but has existed since the very inception of discussions of this issue. I therefore include opinions that both permit and forbid Muslims to live in medieval Spain after it had been conquered by Christians; opinions that both permit and forbid Muslims to live under British rule in India; and opinions that both permit and forbid Muslims to live under the rule of the French in Algeria.

The diversity of the jurists' responses can be seen as a product of their different assessments of what will benefit the Muslim community, and their opinions are consequently deeply sensitive to the sociopolitical predicament of the Muslims they discuss. As can be seen from the texts included in this volume, the jurists who wrote about Muslims under non-Muslim rule do not seem to have felt great pressure to conform to the orthodoxies of their legal schools.[30] They were always careful to situate their responses in the context of their tradition, but this did not hamper them in creating unique responses to the new situations which arose.

The international scope of this anthology is deliberate. When Muslims seek answers to questions about life under non-Muslim rule today, they are not restricted to requesting answers from religious authorities who happen to reside in their countries but are entitled to seek help from authorities whom they trust regardless of where they are located. Although this phenomenon has become more common during the modern period, it is not a new one. Thus, for example, the Egyptian jurist al-Ramlī (957/1550), whose fatwā is translated in this anthology, answered a question about Muslims living in Christian Spain; another Egyptian, Ibn Ḥajar al-Haytamī (d. 973/1567), wrote about Muslims living under non-Muslim rule in India; and the Tunisian jurist ʿAlī b. Muḥammad al-Qābisī

30. It has been sometimes observed that jurists of the Sunnī Mālikī school tend to be less permissive about Muslims living under non-Muslim rule than those of the other legal schools. This position, however, is more a product of their geographic location on the frontier with Christendom and less a product of a desire to conform to a particular legal orthodoxy. See Alan Verskin, "Early Islamic Legal Responses to Living under Christian Rule: Reconquista-Era Development and 19th-Century Impact in the Maghrib (Ph.D. diss.: Princeton University, 2010), 77 ff.

(d. 403/1012) wrote about the situation in the Sudan.[31] In the modern period, perhaps beginning with Rashīd Riḍā (d. 1354/1935), seekers of fatwās became yet more international. Riḍā, who was based in Egypt, received questions from areas as far flung as Europe, China, India, and North America. This trend has become yet more pronounced as more and more fatwās come to be issued on internet websites.

Notes on These Translations

ARABIC NAMES: To the reader unfamiliar with Arabic, Arabic names can seem long and mystifying. Consider the following fictional name as an example: Ḥujjat al-Islām Abū Isḥāq Maḥmūd Ibn Aḥmad al-Baghdādī. *Ḥujjat al-Islām* is a sobriquet (*laqab*), in this case, an honorific meaning "Proof of Islam." Abū Isḥāq is the agnomen (*kunya*), meaning "father of Isḥāq." Maḥmūd is the personal name (*ism*). Ibn Aḥmad is the patronymic (*nasab*), meaning "son of Aḥmad." Sometimes several patronymics occur within a name to indicate grandfathers, great-grandfathers, and so on. Al-Baghdādī is the relative name (*nisba*) which, in this case, means that the individual derives from the city of Baghdad.

DATES: In this anthology, Gregorian dates follow Islamic (*hijrī*) ones. The Islamic calendar begins in the year A.D. 622, the year of the Prophet's migration (*hijra*) from Mecca to Medina.

LEGAL SOURCES: This anthology studies the works of Sunnī Muslim jurists. These jurists were divided into many legal schools of which only four have survived into the modern period. These schools, which have been named for their founders, are the Mālikī, Ḥanafī, Shāfiʿī, and Ḥanbalī schools. Despite their differing on matters of practice and theory, relations between these Sunnī schools have nearly always been characterized by mutual toler-

31. Aḥmad b. Yaḥyā al-Wansharīsī, *al-Miʿyār al-muʿrib wa'l-jāmiʿ al-mughrib ʿan fatāwā ahl Ifrīqiya wa'l-Andalus wa'l-Maghrib*, ed. Muḥammad Ḥajjī (Rabat: Wizārat al-Awqāf wa'l-Shu'ūn al-Islāmīyya li'l-Mamlaka al-Maghribiyya, 1981), 10: 135.

ance. In the modern period, some reformist strands of Islam have attempted to create a jurisprudence independent of the classical schools. Recent fatwās tend to be written in less technical language than those of the past, which were written for a smaller audience that was more steeped in the discipline of Islamic law. Medieval writers of fatwās usually assumed that their readers were not only familiar with the details of the case at hand but also had a basic grasp of Islamic law. As a result, a fatwā was often given in note form with incomplete quotations of texts and with references to sources, people, and places in the most minimal notation. Such hints would be all the original audience needed to understand the import of the argument. Readers of this anthology will be aware of this when they compare al-Wansharīsī's fifteenth-century fatwā with al-ʿAlwānī's twentieth-century one. I have attempted to lessen the reader's difficulties in this regard by providing explanations and completed quotations either in the footnotes or in square brackets. However, out of fealty to my sources, I have avoided the temptation to transform the texts into something more readable by paraphrasing or supplementing the main body of the text.[32]

Legal texts are often difficult to read for those untrained in Islamic law. However, focusing on the texts' legal aspects is not the only option for the reader of this anthology. One social and literary critic once remarked that "there are many ways to read legal opinions, and not all of them are investigations of law." The "lawyerly" way of reading texts, he says, "misses too much about life, and even about law. It can become an obstacle to a full understanding of social developments." It is thus possible, and perhaps even desirable, to try to read these texts "untechnically . . . as documents of ideas, of philosophical and political conceptions, of historical interpretations. It is as such documents that some of them exert their most lasting influence upon society."[33] Therefore, although the legal mechanisms the jurists use to reach their conclusions are important, the reader can gain much by comparing

32. Translations are my own unless otherwise indicated.
33. Leon Wieseltier, "Two Sentences," *The New Republic*, August 2, 2012, 48.

and contrasting the considerations, fears, and hopes that are foremost in the petitioners' minds and in the minds of the *muftīs*. In so doing, rather than seeing the texts merely as a part of the history of law, they can see them as intimate intellectual portraits of Muslims at crisis points in their history.

— 1 —

The End of Muslim Spain

The Christian conquest of Muslim Andalusia, commonly referred to as the Reconquista,[1] left an unprecedentedly large number of Muslims living under Christian rule. Although skirmishes with Christian kingdoms had occurred from the very inception of Muslim rule (circa 92/711), the Reconquista itself is usually said to have begun towards the end of the fifth/eleventh century with the annexation of the Muslim towns of Toledo, which fell in 478/1085, and Huesca, which fell in 489/1096. After these victories, Christian expansion was held back for some time by two successive Maghribī dynasties, the Almoravids and the Almohads, which managed to reconquer some lost territory. However, in the seventh/thirteenth century, with the decline of the Almohads, Christian forces gained momentum and, by the end of the ninth/fifteenth century, Christians had not only ousted all Muslim rulers from al-Andalus, but also controlled most of the Moroccan coast.[2]

Although some Muslims fled from the newly Christian Spain, many still remained. The latter came to be known as the Mudéjars,

1. The term "Reconquista" is problematic because of the narrative of a unified Christian Spain that it assumes. In the absence of an alternative convenient term, however, most historians have chosen to retain it and I have followed their example. Many modern Arabic writers use the term *istirdād*, which is a direct translation of "reconquista," see Muḥammad al-Sharīf, *al-Maghrib wa-ḥurūb al-istirdād* (Tetouan: Jāmiʿat ʿAbd al-Mālik al-Saʿdī, Kulliyyat al-Ādāb wa'l-ʿUlūm al-Insāniyya, 2005). For a discussion of the term "Reconquista" and the debate regarding its use, see Joseph O'Callaghan, *Reconquest and Crusade in Medieval Spain* (Philadelphia: University of Pennsylvania Press, 2003), 3 ff.

2. Andrew Hess, *The Forgotten Frontier: A History of the Sixteenth-Century Ibero-African Frontier* (Chicago: University of Chicago Press, 1978), 6 ff.

in Arabic, *mudajjanūn* or *ahl al-dajn*. Leonard Harvey defines the word as meaning "a Muslim who, after the surrender of a territory to a Christian ruler, remained there without changing religion, and entered into a relationship of vassalage under a Christian king."[3] Some of these Mudéjar communities flourished for as long as several hundred years after their conquests. Some remained because they were compelled by Christian authorities to do so, but it is important to note that many remained there by choice. While Muslims were certainly subject to legal restrictions and intermittent persecutions during much of this period, their initial treatment by Christians can be described as being relatively benign. Over time, as Christian rulers increased their control over these areas and their need for their Muslim subjects therefore diminished, their treatment of the Mudéjars worsened. The matter was brought to a head with the capture of Granada in 897/1492, which completed the Christian conquest of Spain and began the process of the expulsion of its Muslim residents. However, even after the fall of Granada, it seemed as though the status of Muslims as relatively well-tolerated minorities would continue. The rights of Granadan Muslims were guaranteed by a capitulation agreement which, although placing certain restrictions on them, allowed them to continue to practice their religion.[4] In 1498, however, the Archbishop of Toledo, Francisco Jiménez de Cisneros, initiated a change in policy towards the Mudéjars by spearheading a program of mass forced conversion.[5] This new policy provoked a series of Mudéjar revolts throughout the country which were forcibly quelled by Christian forces. The failure of these revolts resulted in a new wave of both conversion to Christianity, under various degrees of compulsion,

3. L. P. Harvey, *Islamic Spain, 1250 to 1500*, 3. The precise derivation of the word Mudéjar is the subject of debate. Scholars have offered several derivations which plausibly relate the word to both Arabic and Spanish roots. On this debate, see F. Maíllo Salgado, "Acerca del uso, significado y referente del término mudéjar," in *Actas del IV congreso internacional encuentro de las tres culturas, Toledo 30 septiembre-2 octubre 1985*, ed. Carlos Carrete Parrondo (Toledo: Tel Aviv University and the city of Toledo, 1988), 103-112.

4. Miguel Angel Ladero Quesada, *Granada después de la conquista: repobladores y mudéjares*, 2nd ed. (Granada: Diputación Provincial de Granada, 1993), 435 ff.

5. David Coleman, *Creating Christian Granada: Society and Religious Culture in an Old-World Frontier City, 1492-1600* (Ithaca: Cornell University Press, 2003), 6.

and of migration, mostly to the Maghrib.[6] These events marked the end of the Mudéjar era. From this period onwards, historians refer to the Muslims who remained in Spain not as Mudéjars, but as "Moriscos,"[7] a term which describes those Muslims who were forced to convert to Christianity, but who continued to practice Islam in secret under political conditions in which Islam and its ritual practices were outlawed. The Moriscos were gradually expelled in a series of waves, the last of which ended in 1614.

Al-Wansharīsī on the Leader of the Muslims of Christian Marbella

The following fatwā on Muslims living under Christian rule was written near the very end of the Mudéjar period by the jurist Aḥmad b. Yaḥyā al-Wansharīsī (d. 914/1508), who is primarily known as the author of a voluminous and influential anthology of Iberian and Maghribī fatwās which date from the fourth/tenth century to his own time.[8] The fatwā concerns the Muslims of the southern Spanish town of Marbella which fell to the Christians in 1485. It discusses whether the Muslim leader of Marbella can continue to live under Christian rule or whether Islamic law mandates that he has to migrate to Islamic territory. The questions are written by Abū ʿAbdallāh Ibn Quṭiyya,[9] about whom nothing is known.

6. On the migration of Muslims to the Maghrib, see M. Marín, "Des migrations forcées: les ʿulema d'al-Andalus face à conquête chrétienne," in *L'Occident musulman et l'Occident chrétien au moyen âge*, ed. M. Hammam (Rabat: Faculté des Lettres, 1995), 44 ff. and J. Vallvé, "La emigración andalusí al Magreb en el siglo XIII," in *Relaciones de la Península Ibérica con el Magreb*, ed. M. García-Arenal and M. J. Viguera (Madrid: Consejo Superior de Investigaciones Científicas, 1988), 87-129.

7. On the problematic nature of this term, see L. P. Harvey, *Muslims in Spain, 1500 to 1614* (Chicago: University of Chicago Press, 2005), 3 ff.

8. On Aḥmad b. Yaḥyā b. Muḥammad b. ʿAbd al-Wāḥid b. ʿAlī al-Wansharīsī, see Francisco Vidal Castro, "Aḥmad al-Wanšarīsī (m. 914/1508). Principales aspectos de su vida," *al-Qanṭara* 12 (1991), 315-52. On al-Wansharīsī's anthology, see F. Vidal Castro, "El Miʿyâr de al-Wanšarîsî (m. 914/1508). I: fuentes, manuscritos, ediciones, traducciones," *Miscelánea de estudios árabes y hebraicos* 42-3 (1993-94), 317-362 and idem, "El Miʿyâr de al-Wanšarîsî (m. 914/1508) II: contenido," *Miscelánea de estudios árabes y hebraicos*, 44 (1995), 213-246. On the influence of al-Wansharīsī, see Jacques Berque, "Ville et université, aperçu sur l'histoire de l'école de Fès," *Revue historique de droit française et étranger* 27 (1949), 89-90.

9. The vocalization of his name is uncertain.

Al-Wansharīsī: On the Leader of the Muslims of Christian Marbella[10]
(after 1486)

[Question]

Praise God, and blessings and peace on the Messenger of God. My master, please give your response to a case, may God be pleased with you and may He, through your life, bring joy to the Muslims.

The case concerns a Marbellan man, well-known for his virtue and piety, who rather than migrating together with his fellow townspeople, stayed behind in order to search for his brother who went missing while fighting the enemy in the land of war. He had until now searched for news of him but, not discovering any and despairing of him, was on the point of migrating when another obstacle arose. This [obstacle] was that he had become a spokesman and helper for the Muslim subject peoples (*dhimmiyyūn*) amongst whom he lived and also for their neighbors who lived in similar circumstances in Western Andalusia. He represented them before the Christian rulers regarding whatever hardships fate dealt them, argued on their behalf, and frequently rescued them from great difficulties. Most of them are unable to perform these [services] themselves. If he were to migrate, few would be found to match him in this art. On account of his loss [of a brother], he had joined them, but the loss of him [the man himself] would cause them great harm. On the grounds that his residing there is of social benefit (*maslaḥa*) to those poor subject peoples, is it possible to grant him a dispensation to live under the rule of the unbelievers, even though he has the ability to migrate whenever he wills it? Or can one give no dispensation to him since [these subject peoples] also have no dispensation for residing there while subject to the laws of unbelief? This is especially the case given that they have been given

10. al-Wansharīsī, *al-Miʿyār al-muʿrib,* 2: 137-141.

permission [by the Christians] to migrate, and most of them have the ability to do so when they wish. [Further], if he were to be given a dispensation [to live there], would he also be given a dispensation to pray in his garments [in whatever degree of purity] he is able [to keep them]? This [would be required] because his clothing would mostly not be free of impurities on account of his aforementioned frequent mixing with Christians, moving about among them, and sleeping and residing in their homes while in the service of the Muslim subject peoples.[11]

Explain for us God's ruling regarding this. If God wills it, may you be praised and rewarded and may abundant peace and the mercy and blessings of God, may He be exalted, support your exalted station.

[Answer]

He [al-Wansharīsī] answered him thus:

Praise is to God alone, here is the answer [to your question], and it is God who bestows success through His grace. It is our one and victorious God who has set the poll-tax (*jizya*)[12] and abasement upon the necks of the accursed unbelievers as chains and fetters with which to roam about the land, cities, and towns, displaying the might of Islam and the nobility of the chosen prophet. Therefore, if one of the Muslims, may God guard and protect them, tries to invert these chains and fetters [by setting them] upon his own neck, he has acted against God and His messenger and has exposed himself to the anger of the Almighty and the Omnipotent. Indeed, it

11. On views of how ritual impurity was transmitted from non-Muslims to Muslims, see Janina Safran, "Rules of Purity and Confessional Boundaries: Mālikī Debates about the Pollution of the Christian," *History of Religions* 42 (2003), 204; Z. Maghen, "Close Encounters: Some Preliminary Observations on the Transmission of Impurity in Early Sunnī Jurisprudence," *Islamic Law and Society* 6 (1999), 348-392; and idem, "Strangers and Brothers: The Ritual Status of Unbelievers in Islamic Jurisprudence," *Medieval Encounters* 12 (2006), 173-223.

12. The *jizya* or poll-tax is the tax levied upon people of the book. On its origin and function, see Claude Cahen, "Djizya," in *The Encyclopedia of Islam, 2nd ed.*, 2: 559–62.

would be fitting for God to hurl him together with them into Hellfire: "God has decreed: I shall conquer, I and My messengers. God is Strong and Almighty" (Qur'ān 58: 21). It is obligatory for every believer with faith in God and the Last Day to endeavor to preserve this basic principle of faith by distancing himself and fleeing from the dwellings of the enemies of the Merciful One's ally [i.e., the Prophet].

To make excuses for the aforementioned virtuous man because of his intention of acting as an interpreter between the tyrant and his sinful Mudéjar[13] subjects does not free him from the obligation of migration. No one should be under the delusion that there is [any genuine] opposition to the obligation [of migration] in the prescriptions for evading it noted in the question – except someone who displays feigned or genuine ignorance of this inversion of Islam (*fiṭra*), or who has no knowledge of the sources from which the law is derived. Dwelling among the unbelievers, other than those who are protected and humbled peoples (*ahl al-dhimma wa'l-ṣaghār*), is not permitted and is not allowed for so much as an hour of a day. This is because of the filth, dirt, and religious and worldly corruption which is ever-present [among them].

[A list of factors precluding Muslims from living in the abode of unbelief]

[1] Among these is that the purpose of Divine Law is for the word of Islam and witness to the truth to be raised high above all others, free from scorn and from the banners of unbelief triumphing over it. Their dwelling in humiliation and abasement necessitates that this noble, exalted and sublime word be abased rather than sublime, and be disdained rather than holy. [Knowing about] this violation of the Law's principles

13. Arabic: *Ahl al-dajn*. A Mudéjar is defined as "a Muslim who, after the surrender of a territory to a Christian ruler, remained there without changing religion, and entered into a relationship of vassalage under a Christian king." L. P. Harvey, *Islamic Spain, 1250 to 1500*, 3.

and foundations and about the one who, without necessity or compulsion, spends his life patiently enduring it, should be sufficient for you [to understand the position of the Law].

[2] Among these is the [issue of the] fulfillment of prayer, the fulfillment of which is second in virtue [only] to the two Declarations of Faith. Glorifying [God] and conducting prayer publicly cannot occur, or [even] be imagined to occur, except in an environment in which [Islam] is entirely out in the open, exalted, and free from scorn and contempt. However, dwelling among the unbelievers and intimately associating with the iniquitous exposes [Islam] to humiliation, disdain, derision and jest. God, may He be exalted, said: "When you make the call to prayer, they take it for a jest and sport. That is because they are a people who do not understand" (Qur'ān 5:58).

[3] Among these is almsgiving (*zakāt*). It is clear to one who possesses understanding and an enlightened mind that, according to the basic tenets of Islam and the ordinances of all humankind, the collection of alms is the responsibility of the ruler. Where there is no ruler, because of the absence of this necessary condition, there is no collection of alms. There can be no alms because of the absence of the person who is entitled to collect it. This basic tenet of Islam is demolished by accepting the rule of unbelievers. As for [alms] being collected by someone who will use them against the Muslims, it is clear that this also involves opposing all the acts of worship mandated by the Law

[4] Among these is the fast of the month of Ramaḍān – which is clearly a duty incumbent upon every Muslim – as well as the alms given at the end of that month. The beginning and end [of the fast of Ramaḍān] are conditional on the sighting of the new moon. Under most circumstances this sighting can only be established by a witness's testimony, and this testimony cannot be given except before Muslim rulers or their

deputies. Where there is no Muslim ruler or deputy, there can be no testimony by witnesses. Therefore, with respect to legal practice, the [precise] beginning and end of the month is uncertain.

[5] Among these is pilgrimage to the House [the *ḥajj* pilgrimage to Mecca]. [Muslims] are still charged with performing the *ḥajj* pilgrimage even if this obligation is suspended because of their lack of ability to do so.

[6] The jihād for elevating the word of truth and annihilating unbelief is one of the basic tenets of Islamic practice. It is an obligation on the Muslim community as a whole (*farḍ ʿalā al-kifāya*), should the necessity arise, especially in the place of residence and vicinity in question. If their abandonment of jihād is not out of absolute necessity, then they are like someone who, out of no necessity, resolves to abandon [the obligation of] migration; and someone who determines to do so without necessity is like someone who freely and intentionally abandons it. As for those who defiantly pursue the opposite [of jihād] by aiding their [Christian] allies against the Muslims, either with their lives or their property, they, together with the polytheists, have the status of enemy combatants. This opposition [to the truth] and error should be sufficient for you [to understand the position of the Law].

This account has made it clear that the prayers, fasts, alms, and jihād [of Muslim residents of the abode of unbelief] are deficient. It indicates that they transgress by not exalting the word of God and witness to the truth and, [on the contrary], neglect to bring it to light, glorify it and elevate it above the scorn of the unbelievers and the derision of the iniquitous. How could a jurist or pious person hesitate to forbid a residence [in the abode of unbelief] which involves opposition to all of these noble and sublime Islamic principles, together with the worldly degradation, abasement and humiliation that living in subjection generally involves. It moreover offends against the well-known glory of the Muslims and against their exalted rank by inciting people to despise and oppress the religion (*dīn*) [of Islam]. These are indeed matters which make one's ears ring.

[7] Among these is the humiliation, scorn and belittlement regarding which the Prophet, peace be upon him, has said: "It is incumbent on a Muslim not to abase himself,"[14] and he [also] said: "The upper hand is better than the lower hand."[15]

[8] Among these is the scorn and mockery [of the unbelievers] which no one possessed of virtuous manliness (*murūwa*) would endure unless compelled by necessity.

[9] Among these is the belittlement and harm to his honor, and perhaps also to his person and property. It is clear what this involves from the perspective of the Sunna and manliness.

[10] Among these is becoming engrossed in viewing objectionable things, being subjected to contact with ritual pollutants, eating forbidden things, and the like.

[11] Among these are the treaty violations by the [Christian] king and [his] control over life, wife, children and property, which are to be anticipated with dread.

ʿUmar b. ʿAbd al-ʿAzīz[16] gave an account of the prohibition against residing in the Andalusian peninsula. He did this despite it being, at that time, a frontier fortress, the virtue of which no one can be ignorant,[17] and despite the fact that the

14. See, for example, *Jāmiʿ al-Tirmidhī* (Cairo: Dār al-Ḥadīth, 2001), n. 2204.

15. *Ṣaḥīḥ al-Bukhārī*, no. 1427.

16. This is the Umayyad caliph (r. 99/717 to 101/720) who, according to tradition, is renowned for his piety, see *Encyclopedia of Islam*, 2nd ed., s.v., "ʿUmar (II) b. ʿAbd al-Azīz."

17. On the frontier fortress (*ribāṭ*) and its virtue, see Majid Khadduri, *War and Peace in the Law of Islam* (Baltimore: Johns Hopkins University Press, 1955), 81-82.

Muslims there had power, ascendancy, plentiful numbers and provisions. Despite all of this, the caliph of the time, whose virtue, piety, righteousness and good counsel of his subjects is agreed upon, prohibited [residence in Andalusia] out of fear of corruption. How much more so would this be the case regarding one who throws himself, his wife, and his children into their hands when they are powerful and ascendant and supported with great numbers and plentiful provisions, and then depends on them to fulfill their pacts in [accordance with] their law. [In contrast], we do not [even] accept their testimony as valid when it is given about themselves, let alone when it is given about us.[18] How can we rely on their claim to fulfill [their pact], given what has already happened and given the events to which anyone who investigates and examines reports of the region can attest?

[12] Among these, even if one assumes that their kings and notables will fulfill [their treaties], are fears for life, wife, children and also property, on account of their wicked people, fools and murderers. Their customs also bear witness to this and events confirm it.

[13] Among these is fear of religious corruption. Even if one concedes that those distinguished in wisdom might be secure [in their faith], who would there be to safeguard the young, the fools, the weak and the women when the notables and devils of the enemy call upon them?

[14] Among these is corruption through sexual relations. How will anyone who has a wife, daughter or pretty female relative safeguard her from a vulgar person from among the enemy's dogs or faithless pigs chancing upon her, and then beguiling and deceiving her respecting her religion? He would over-

18. On the law regarding the acceptance or non-acceptance of the testimony of non-Muslims, see Antoine Fattal, *Le Statut légal des non-Musulmans en pays d'Islam* (Beirut: Imprimerie Catholique, 1958), 361 ff.

power her and she would be obedient to him, making apostasy and religious corruption separate her from her guardian. This resembles what happened to al-Muʿtamad Ibn ʿAbbād's daughter-in-law and her children,[19] may God guard us against affliction and the enemies' malicious gloating.

[15] Among these is the spread of their reprehensible way of life, language, dress and customs to those who have lived among them for years. This is what happened to the people of Ávila[20] and of other such places who have lost knowledge of the Arabic language entirely. When knowledge of the Arabic language is entirely lost,[21] acts of worship are also lost. How can one even consider the abandonment of the verbal acts of worship which are so abundant in number and virtue?

[16] Among these is fear of [the unbelievers'] taking control over property by instituting heavy levies and unjust taxes. This leads to them expropriating property completely by encompassing it in the taxes of unbelief, whether all at once, on the pretext of some passing necessity, or through many payments. Or it might be that [their expropriations] rely upon some invented excuse or interpretation which it is impossible to make them reconsider or debate – even if these excuses are supremely weak, clearly feeble and corrupt. They [the Mudéjars] do not have the audacity to do anything about this lest their actions cause the kindling of hatred and lead to the abrogation of the treaty [with the consequence that the Chris-

---

19. The daughter-in-law of al-Muʿtamad b. ʿAbbād (r. 462-84/1069- 1091), the last ruler of the ʿAbbādid dynasty, is reported to have become the mistress of King Alphonso VI of Castille and to have converted to Christianity. On this event, see E. Lévi-Provençal, "La 'mora Zaida', femme d'Alphonse VI de Castille et leur fils l'infant D. Sancho," *Hesperis* 18 (1934), 1-8.

20. It has been plausibly suggested that the text refers not to Ávila but to Ayelo in Valencia, see P. S. van Koningsveld and G. A. Wiegers, "The Islamic Statute of the Mudéjars in the Light of a New Source," *al-Qanṭara* 17 (1996), 28.

21. On the issue of the loss of the Arabic language, see Gerard Wiegers, "Language and Identity: Pluralism and the Use of Non-Arabic Languages in the Muslim West," in *Pluralism and Identity: Studies in Ritual Behaviour*, ed. Jan Platvoet et al. (Leiden: Brill, 1995), 303 ff. and John Boswell, *The Royal Treasure* (New Haven: Yale University Press, 1977), 303 ff.

tians] will take control of their lives, wives and children. Events bear witness to this for one who has examined them. This has even occurred many times in the place in question as well as in other places.

These present and anticipated corruptions firmly support the prohibition of residence [in the abode of unbelief] and the ban of this perversion of what is right. The different factors involved lead to a single conclusion. The leading jurists have already expanded this basic rule to other situations because of its strength and the clarity of its prohibition. The imām of Medina (*dār al-hijra*), Abū ʿAbdallāh Mālik b. Anas (d. 179/795), may God be pleased with him, said: "The Qurʾānic verses on migration teach that every Muslim must leave lands in which normative practices (*sunan*) are altered and in which other than what is right is in force," not to speak of leaving and fleeing from the lands of unbelief and the places of the iniquitous. God forbid that a virtuous and monotheistic community, while glorifying and praising God, be dependent on trinitarians and be content to dwell amongst impurity and filth. There is no scope for the aforementioned, virtuous [Marbellan] man to remain in the aforementioned place for [his] aforementioned objective. No dispensation can be given to him or to his companions regarding whatever impurities and pollutants attach themselves to their clothing and bodies. This is because pardon for these [impurities] is conditional upon the difficulty in guarding and protecting against these things and no such difficulty can attach to their choice of residing [in the abode of unbelief] and acting against what is right. God, may He be exalted, knows best and it is He who gives success.

This was written, with greetings to those for whom there is no God but God, by the poor and wretched slave who seeks God's forgiveness and desires blessings for one who applies himself to this [fatwā] and carries it out.

ʿUbaydallāh Aḥmad b. Yaḥyā
b. Muḥammad b. ʿAlī al-Wansharīsī

Al-Ramlī on the Muslims of Christian Spain

Shihāb al-Dīn Abū al-ʿAbbās Aḥmad al-Ramlī (d. 957/1550) was one of the most prominent Egyptian Shāfiʿī jurists of his day. He was also the father of Shams al-Dīn al-Ramlī, who was given the honorific "The Little Shāfiʿī," to indicate that he had been recognized as the greatest judicial authority of his age. The latter collected his father's fatwās and it is from this volume that the text below is drawn.[22] It is difficult to date this fatwā with precision. Given, however, that it speaks favorably of Christian tolerance in Aragon and that, in 1526, a policy of forced baptism of Aragonese Muslims was imposed, one can assume that the question to which al-Ramlī responded preceded this date.[23] Shāfiʿī jurists like al-Ramlī tend to be more permissive of Muslims living in non-Muslim territory. This is likely because the founder of their school permitted Muslims to live in such lands provided that they were not subject to enticement away from religion.[24]

Al-Ramlī: On the Muslims of Christian Spain[25]
(early tenth/sixteenth century)

[Question]

This question concerns Muslims dwelling in a region of Andalusia called Aragon, who are under the pact of protection of a Christian ruler. [This ruler] takes the land tax (*kharāj*) from them in proportion to what they earn but, other than that, he has not wronged them either with respect to their property or their persons. They have mosques in which they

22. On the younger al-Ramlī, see A. Zysow, *Encyclopedia of Islam*, 2nd ed. s.v., "al-Ramlī."

23. On the Morisco community of Aragon, see William Monter, *Frontiers of Heresy: The Spanish Inquisition from the Basque Lands to Sicily* (Cambridge: Cambridge University Press, 2002), 189-230.

24. Abou El Fadl, "Islamic Law and Muslim Minorities," 147 ff.

25. Shams al-Dīn al-Ramlī, *Fatāwā* (Cairo:ʿAbd al-Ḥamīd Aḥmad al-Ḥanafī, 1938), 52-54.

pray, they fast on Ramaḍān, give alms and redeem prisoners from the Christians if they are able. They publically uphold the Islamic penalties (*ḥudūd*) as is appropriate and they visibly manifest the fundamentals of Islam (*qawāʿid al-Islām*) as is obligatory. The Christians do not interfere at all in their religious acts and they [the Muslims] pray for the Muslim rulers in their sermons (*khuṭab*) without specifying which one, and beseech God to grant them victory and to destroy their enemies, the unbelievers. In spite of this, they fear that they sin by residing in the lands of the unbeliever. Is migration obligatory for them [in a place] where public manifestation of religion [is permitted], given that they have no assurance against being compelled to apostatize – God, may He be exalted, save us – or having their [the unbelievers'] laws applied to them? Or is [migration] not obligatory for them given their aforementioned situation?

If a man from the aforementioned region carries out the obligation of the *ḥajj* pilgrimage without the permission of his parents, out of fear that they will prevent him from it, is his pilgrimage valid? Is his return to his parents in the aforementioned region permissible?

[Answer]

Because of their ability to manifest their religion, migration from this region is not obligatory for Muslims. [It is not obligatory] because [the Prophet], may God bless him and grant him peace, sent ʿUthmān[26] to Mecca on the day [of the treaty] of al-Ḥudaybiyya,[27] because he was able to publically manifest his religion there. He did not permit migration to them [the Meccans] because he hoped that, by residing there, others would convert to Islam. On account of this it [Mecca] was an "abode of Islam" – if they were to migrate from it, it

26. ʿUthmān b. ʿAffān (d. 35/655), a companion of the Prophet and the third caliph.

27. The treaty of al-Ḥudaybiyya was a temporary truce that the Prophet made with the Meccans in 6/628. Mecca was conquered by the Muslims in 8/630.

would become an abode of war. As for what is mentioned in the question about their publically manifesting the laws of the pure *Sharīʿa*, and the unbeliever's lack of interference with them on account of it for the duration of many years, it can likely be inferred from this that they are secure from compulsion to apostatize from Islam and from the application of the unbeliever's laws upon them. And God knows best how to tell harm from benefit.

As for the man leaving to perform the *ḥajj* pilgrimage obligation without the permission of his parents, there is no objection to this. This is because, as is the case with prayer and fasts, it is not the parent's right to prevent him from performing the obligatory *ḥajj* – whether from beginning it or from completing it. It is permissible for him after he has performed its rites to return to his parents in the aforementioned region, and his obligation is regarded as having been validly discharged.

— 2 —

Rulers Who Falsely Claim to Be Muslims

Ibn Taymiyya on the Town of Mārdīn under the Mongols

Taqī al-Dīn Ibn Taymiyya (d. 728/1328), a prominent and prolific Ḥanbalī scholar, lived most of his life in Syria and Egypt.[1] Although a leading intellectual figure of his day, his strident religious and political views led on several occasions to his imprisonment. Several of Ibn Taymiyya's fatwās are written against the Mongols[2] who posed a military threat to the Mamlūk society in which he lived. In his fatwās, Ibn Taymiyya accuses the Mongols of being unbelievers. He acknowledges that they have outwardly converted to Islam but says that these conversions are insincere and are therefore not to be taken into account. His major basis for challenging the sincerity of their belief was that the Mongols had instituted their own legal code in preference to Islamic law.[3] In the fatwā that I have translated below, the focus is not on the Mongols themselves but on the status of Muslims who have been conquered by them. The fatwā concerns the town of Mārdīn, located in present-day

1. On his life, see Yossef Rapoport and Shahab Ahmed (eds.), *Ibn Taymiyya and His Times* (New York: Oxford University Press, 2010).

2. He refers to them as the Tatars.

3. Reuven Amitai-Preiss, "Ghazan, Islam and Mongol Tradition: A View from the Mamlūk Sultanate," *Bulletin of the School of Oriental and African Studies* 59 (1996), 1-10 and Denise Aigle, "The Mongol Invasions of Bilād al-Shām by Ghāzān Khān and Ibn Taymīyah's Three "Anti-Mongol" Fatwas," *Mamlūk Studies Review* 11 (2007), 89-120.

southeastern Turkey near the Syrian border, which had come under Mongol control in the second half of the seventh/thirteenth century.

Ibn Taymiyya's Mārdīn fatwā is frequently referred to in modern jihādist literature.[4] This is largely because of Ibn Taymiyya's answer to the question of whether the town is an abode of peace or an abode of war. He avoids placing it in either category, but says that Mārdīn is a place in which "a Muslim is treated according to what he deserves and the one who deviates from Islamic law is treated (variant: fought)[5] according to what he deserves." Ibn Taymiyya achieves two objectives by creating this intermediate category between the abode of peace and the abode of war. If Mārdīn is an abode of peace, its ruler would be regarded as Islamic and would have a monopoly on the use of warfare. Those dissatisfied with him would have no license to express that dissatisfaction by declaring jihād. If, on the other hand, the land was an abode of war, Mārdīn's ruler would not be regarded as legitimate and it would be permissible to wage jihād against him. However, Muslims would also not be permitted to live permanently in such territory and would have attenuated property rights. Since Ibn Taymiyya is dissatisfied with the instability caused by the latter categorization and the justification of the Mongols given by the former categorization, he creates an intermediate category between the two in which Muslims can still redress the wrongs of the Mongol ruler but in which the general stability of the society is maintained. The intermediate category reduces the authority of the ruler while still keeping in place most of the laws which govern an Islamic society. Ibn Taymiyya's statement has been seized upon by contemporary groups who seek to justify activities against nominally Islamic states that they deem to be acting un-Islamically.[6]

---

4. Gilles Kepel, *Muslim Extremism in Egypt* (Berkeley: University of California, 1985), 195.

5. It is the variant "fought" which appears in most printed editions. Which variant Ibn Taymiyya intended is the subject of debate.

6. For the fatwā's contemporary treatment, see Yahya Michot, "Ibn Taymiyya's "New Mardin Fatwa". Is Genetically Modified Islam (GMI) Carcinogenic?" *The Muslim World* 101 (2011), 130-81. The article reflects Michot's own participation in some of the events that he describes.

In March 2010, an international group of leading Islamic intellectuals convened in the town of Mārdīn to deal with the implications of this fatwā.[7] The conference produced a declaration which offered a novel interpretation of the fatwā. What the fatwā taught, they said, was that it was possible to go beyond the traditional division of the world into an abode of Islam and an abode of war. This insight, they said, could thus provide a blueprint for peaceful relations between Muslim and non-Muslim countries. The declaration reads:

> Ibn Taymiyya, in his classification of the city of Mardin… went beyond the classification that was common amongst past Muslim jurists: Dividing territories into an *Abode of Islam* (in which the primary state is peace), an *Abode of Kufr* (Unbelief) (in which the primary state is war), and an *Abode of 'Ahd* (Covenant) (in which the primary state is truce), amongst other divisions … Instead of the classification common in his age, Ibn Taymiyya came up with a compound/ composite classification by virtue of which civil strife amongst Muslims was averted, and their lives, wealth, and honor safeguarded, and justice amongst them and others established. His fatwa is one that is exceptional in its formulation and that, to a large degree, addresses a similar context to our time, a political state of the world that is different from the one encountered by past jurists, and which had formed the basis for the particular way in which they had classified territories.[8]

Regardless of whether or not one accepts the conveners of the conference's attempt to cast Ibn Taymiyya as a forerunner of a project of reconciliation between Muslim and non-Muslim lands, they are clearly correct in recognizing the creativity of Ibn Taymiyya's

7. The main speakers at the conference were: Ahmad Abidi Arani (Iran), 'Abdallah bin Bayah (Mauritania), Mustafa Cerić (Bosnia), Ayedh al-Dosari (Saudi Arabia), Habib 'Ali al-Jifri (Yemen), Mohamed El Moctar Ould M'Balle (Mauritania), Abdullah Nasseef (Saudi Arabia), Aref Ali Nayed (United Arab Emirates), Ahmet Özel (Turkey), Hani Abdul Shakur (Saudi Arabia), Muhammed Uzair Shams (India) and 'Abd al-Wahhab b. Nasir al-Turayri (Saudi Arabia).

8. "The New Mardin Declaration," accessed June 20, 2012, http://www.mardin-fatwa.com/attach/ Mardin_Declaration_English.pdf.

position in attempting to go beyond a binary distinction between the abode of Islam and the abode of war.

Ibn Taymiyya: On the Status of Mārdīn under the Mongols[9]
(c. 7th/13th century)

[Question]

[Ibn Taymiyya], may God be merciful to him, was questioned regarding the land of Mārdīn: Is it a land of war or a land of peace (*silm*)? Is it obligatory for a Muslim who resides there to migrate to the lands of Islam or not? If migration is obligatory for him and he does not perform it and aids the enemies of the Muslims with his person or property, is he committing a sin? And, does someone who charges him with hypocrisy (*nifāq*) and reviles him sin or not?

[Answer]

He [Ibn Taymiyya] answered: Praise God, the blood and property of Muslims is inviolable whether they live in Mārdīn or elsewhere. Giving aid to those who deviate from Islamic religious law (*sharīʿat dīn al-Islām*) is forbidden, whether they are from Mārdīn or from elsewhere. If someone who resides there [in Mārdīn] is incapable of upholding his religion, it is obligatory for him to migrate. If not,[10] [migration] is recommended, but not obligatory.

It is forbidden for them to help the enemy of the Muslims with their persons and property. They must refrain from this in any way available to them, whether by evasion, equivocation, or dissimulation. If it is not possible [to refrain] except by migrating, then each has an individual obligation to do so.

9. Translated from Ibn Taymiyya, *Majmūʿ fatāwā Shaykh al-Islām Aḥmad Ibn Taymiyya*, ed. ʿAbd al-Raḥmān b. Muḥammad b. Qāsim al-ʿĀṣimī (Riyad: Maṭābiʿ al-Riyāḍ, 1961-67), 28: 240-41.

10. That is, he is capable of upholding his religion.

> In general, one is not permitted to revile them [Mārdīn's Muslim subjects] or charge them with hypocrisy. However, revilement and charging with hypocrisy should proceed according to the ways mentioned in the Book and the *Sunna*. This pertains to the people of Mārdīn and to others.
>
> As for whether it is an abode of war or of peace – it is a combination of both concepts. It does not have the status of the abode of peace in which the laws of Islam apply because there is an army of Muslims [which ensures that they are implemented]. And it does not have the status of the abode of war, the people of which are unbelievers. Rather, it is a third category in which a Muslim is treated according to what he deserves and someone who deviates from Islamic law is treated (variant: fought) according to what he deserves.

ʿUthmān Ibn Fūdī and Hausaland

ʿUthmān Ibn Fūdī (d. 1232/1817), often spelled Usman Dan Fodio, was a descendant of a prominent family of legal scholars in Hausaland, located in present-day Nigeria.[11] The spread of Islam in this region, which likely began in the 14th century, was accomplished by networks of Muslim traders. By the eighteenth century, all rulers of the region were Muslim, but their observance of Islam and that of their subjects was strongly admixed with local customs and beliefs. In 1188/1774, Ibn Fūdī, in the name of promoting a purer Islam, began to preach sermons which attacked both Muslim rulers and the religious leadership for tolerating practices involving religious syncretism. His teachings began to attract a large following which the rulers under whom he lived tried to suppress. After a number of such attempts, Ibn Fūdī declared the land to be no longer a part of the abode of Islam and called for migration (*hijra*). He

11. For his biography, see Mervyn Hiskett, *The Sword of Truth: The Life and Times of the Shehu Usuman Dan Fodio*, 2nd edition (Evanston: Northwestern University Press, 1994).

and his followers then left his former home at Degel for the remote district of Gudu and founded the Caliphate of Sokoto.[12]

Ibn Fūdī's most comprehensive discussion of the doctrine of migration from non-Muslim territory occurs in his *Bayān wujūb al-hijra ʿalā al-ʿibād* (Exposition of the Obligation of Migration for the Servants of God). In this work, he cites many of the classic texts on migration from the Qurʾān and *ḥadīth* which he draws largely from the works of al-Wansharīsī.[13] He adapts al-Wansharīsī's teaching to the political situation of Hausaland by providing a detailed doctrine of the classification of territory. For him, whether a territory is classified as the abode of unbelief is determined not by the religion of its inhabitants, but by the religion of its ruler. Thus, even if there is a territory in which "Islam predominates and unbelief is rare," it cannot be considered a part of the abode of Islam if its ruler is not a Muslim. Moreover, the fact that the ruler claims to be a Muslim is not sufficient to qualify his territory as a part of the abode of Islam if his conduct is un-Islamic. Such rulers, Ibn Fūdī says, although professing Islam, are in fact "polytheists, turning from the path of God and raising the banner of the kingdom of this world above the banner of Islam – and that is all unbelief according to the consensus of the jurists (*ijmāʿ*)."[14] Ibn Fūdī uses his land classification criterion to make it very difficult for a country to qualify as being a part of the abode of Islam with the result that he concludes that all of the Sudan is actually a part of the abode of war and that it is necessary for Muslims to migrate from it.[15]

12. Mervyn Hiskett, *The Sword of Truth*, 9 ff. and Murray Last, *The Sokoto Caliphate* (New York: Humanities Press, 1967), 3-60.

13. ʿUthmān b. Fūdī, *Bayān wujūb al-hijra ʿalā al-ʿibād*, ed. F. H. El Masri (Oxford: Oxford University Press, 1978), 6a.

14. Ibid., 7b.

15. This position was criticized by some of Ibn Fūdī's contemporaries, see Muḥammad Bello, *Infāq al-maysūr* (Legon: Institute of African Studies, University of Ghana, 1964), 157-198 and ʿAbdallāh Ibn Muḥammad al-Turūdī, *Tazyīn al-waraqāt*, ed. M. Hiskett (Ibadan: Ibadan University Press, 1963), 132.

Ibn Fūdī: On the Obligation of Migrating from the Lands of the Unbelievers[16]

(1221/1806)

Translated by F. H. El Masri

I say, and success is from God: Migration from the lands of the unbelievers is an obligation according to the Book,[17] the *Sunna*[18] and consensus (*ijmāʿ*). As for the Book, there is the word of God: "As for those whom the angels take in death while they wrong themselves, [the angels] will ask: In what circumstances were you? They will say: 'We were oppressed in the land.' [The angels] will say: 'Was not God's earth spacious that you could have migrated therein?' As for these, their abode will be hell, an evil journey's end." (Qurʾān 4: 97) The commentators said: "And in this verse is a proof of the obligation of migration from the lands of the unbelievers." Al-Suyūṭī (d. 911/1505) said in his *Takmila*, explaining the meaning of the word of God, "wrong themselves": "[It means] by remaining among the unbelievers and failing to migrate." As for the *Sunna*, there is the saying of the Prophet, "God is quit of a Muslim who dwells among the polytheists", and his saying, "The fires of a believer and an unbeliever should not be within sight of each other." The [above] two *ḥadīth*s were cited by our master al-Kuntī (d. 1226/1811)[19] in his *Naṣīḥa*. There is also the saying of the Prophet, "He who mixes or lives with an unbeliever is just like him." This was related by Abū Dāwūd on the authority of Samura.

As for consensus, al-Wansharīsī said in his *Miʿyār*: "And consensus upholds the obligation of migration."

16. The translation is that of F. H. El Masri, which I have slightly modified, contained in ʿUthmān Ibn Fūdī, *Bayān wujūb al-hijra ʿalā al-ʿibād*, (Khartoum: Khartoum University Press and Oxford University Press, 1978), 48-52.

17. I.e., the Qurʾān.

18. I.e., the statements and behavior of the Prophet Muḥammad.

19. Al-Kuntī was a prominent West African ṣūfī leader, see Aziz Batran, *The Qadiriyya Brotherhood in West Africa and the Western Sahara: The Life and Times of Shaykh al-Mukhtar al-Kunti, (1729-1811)* (Rabat: Publications de l'Institut des études africaines, 2001).

Considerations of blood relationship and marriage should not be an excuse for anyone failing to perform *hijra*. How much less possessions and dwellings! God has said: "Say: If your fathers, your sons, your brothers, your wives, your tribe, and the wealth you have acquired, and the merchandise for which you fear that there will no sale, and dwellings you desire are dearer to you than God and His messenger and striving in His way" — so that you fail to emigrate because of it, as explained in the *Takmila* of al-Suyūṭī, "then wait until God brings His decree."[20] And according to the commentary of al-Khāzin,[21] the occasion of the revelation of this verse were the words of those who accepted Islam but did not migrate: "If we migrate, our possessions will be lost, our commerce wasted, our dwellings ruined and we will have broken our bonds of kin." He [al-Khāzin] then said: "And in this verse there is also a proof that whenever there is a conflict between religious matters and worldly interests, a Muslim is obliged to give preference to the matter of religion over the worldly interests!"

I would add that it is likewise necessary to give preference to its preservation over the rest of the five general principles, which are: [religion], the preservation of life, the intellect, lineage and property; and some also added honor.[22] Al-Laqqānī[23] said in his *Itḥāf* [*al-murīd*] regarding the words of the poet:

And the preservation of religion, life,
property and lineage
And likewise of intellect and honor is obligatory.

The most important of the five is religion, because the preservation of the others is [only] a means of preserving it. Then

20. Qur'ān 9: 24.

21. ʿAlī b. Muḥammad al-Baghdādī (d. 741/1341).

22. For a general outline of these principles, see Bernard Weiss, *Spirit of Islamic Law*, 170.

23. I.e., ʿAbd al-Salām b. Ibrāhīm al-Laqqānī (d. 1078/1668).

comes the preservation of lives, then of intellects, then of lineage, then of property; and of the same importance as the latter is the preservation of honor, so long as injury to it does not lead to breaking bonds of kinship; otherwise it comes on a level with the preservation of lineage." Then he [al-Laqqānī] said: "In all systems of divine law it is essential to preserve all of them because of their noble status."

If you have understood what has gone before, you will realize that according to the Book, the *Sunna* and consensus, one is obliged to migrate from the unbelievers' lands, among which are most of the lands of the Sudan, for its lands fall into three classes as may be understood from the writings of the learned men. One of these is [a land] where unbelief predominates and Islam is rarely found, such as the lands of Mossi, Gurma, Busa, Borgu, Yoruba, Dagomba, Kutukuli, *t.n.b.gh.*, Būbul and *gh.m.b.y.*,[24] according to the examples given by Aḥmad Bābā in his *Kashf.* All these are lands of unbelief without any doubt, for judgment is passed with reference to the majority. Also, all the rulers of lands of this class are unbelievers, and the status of a land is that of its ruler as will be mentioned below, if God wills.

Another class is those lands where Islam predominates and unbelief is rare such as Borno, Kano, Katsina, Songhay and Mali according to the examples given by Aḥmad Bāba (d. 1036/1627) in the aforementioned book. These, too, are lands of unbelief without any doubt, since the spread of Islam there is [only] among the masses, but as for their rulers, they are unbelievers just like [those of] the first division, even though they profess Islam. [That is] because they are polytheists, turning [people] from the path of God and raising the banner of the kingdom of this world above the banner of Islam — and that is all unbelief according to consensus. And it is undisputed that the status of a land is that of its ruler — if the ruler is a Muslim, the land is a land of Islam and if he is an unbeliever, the land is a land of unbelief from which flight

24. The vocalization of these names is uncertain.

(*firār*) is obligatory. On account of this, Aḥmad b. Saʿīd said in his *Mukhtaṣar*: "There is no disagreement about the obligation upon Muslims to depose their leader if he is an unbeliever. But it is only incumbent on them to rise against him if they think they can overcome him, [but] if they realize their inability to do so, they are not obliged to rise against him. However, every Muslim is obliged to migrate from such a ruler's land to somewhere else."

What we have mentioned [above, regarding the fact] that the rulers of this [second] division are unbelievers, is based on what is generally observed about them. This does not mean that some of them may not be Muslims in rare cases, [but] the exception carries no [legal] weight.

The [third] class of lands in the Sudan does not belong to the lands of unbelief either as regards the rulers or as regards the masses, but belongs wholly to the lands of Islam and this class is unknown to us in the lands of the Sudan, but its existence can be inferred from what the learned men have said, as will be shown, if God wills.

Our master, al-Kuntī, said in his *Naṣīḥa*: "The Sudan is a land where unbelief prevails among the majority of its people and all the Muslims there are under the domination of the unbelievers whom they have recognized as rulers. And people generally adopt the behavior of their ruler remaining in the darkness of ignorance, willfulness and unbelief. This is why it is forbidden to travel into the land of enemies and the land of the Sudan. Abū'l-Ḥasan in *Taḥqīq al-mabānī*, a commentary on [Ibn Abī Zayd al-Qayrawānī's (d. 386/996)] *Risāla*, explaining the author's words: "To make trading [journeys] to enemies' lands and to the Sudan is reprehensible," said: "that means [trading journeys to] the unbelievers among them." It amounts to his saying that trading with the land of enemies is reprehensible, be they Sudanese or otherwise. Then he said: "Al-Dāwūdī said, "As for the lands of the Sudan, it has been said that the meaning of this is the lands of unbelief therein." This statement indicates that within the lands of the Sudan are lands of unbelief as well as lands of Islam, as has previously been indicated. And that is the apparent meaning of Aḥmad Bābā's account in his *Kashf*. But I have read in the writings of a certain scholar [a statement] which reports that there are absolutely no lands of Islam in the Sudan. He says therein: "The sultans of the lands of the Sudan, which are lands of unbelief having nothing in common with lands of Islam, have all, one after another, rendered the *Sharīʿa* of our Prophet Muḥammad ineffective."[25] And God knows best.

If you ask whether the Muslims among the people of the Sudan accepted Islam through being conquered or whether they professed it voluntarily, I would say that the answer to this is as was stated by Shaykh Aḥmad Bābā in his *Kashf* when he said: "They accepted Islam without being conquered by anybody." In another place he said: "It appears from what Ibn Khaldūn (d. 808/1406) and others said that those who became Muslims from among the Sudanese did so voluntarily without being conquered by anybody." Again, he said: "One of the Sudanese judges said that the leader who conquered them while they were unbelievers preferred to let them remain as slaves." Then Shaykh Aḥmad Bābā said: "This is something we have never heard of, nor was it transmitted to us; so ask this Sudanese judge who that leader was. When did he conquer their land and which areas did he conquer? Let him specify all that to you. It is very likely that his [the judge's] account is untrue, for if you inquire nowadays you will not find anybody who can confirm the truth of what he said. So what is based on his report cannot be taken into consideration and it appears most likely that it is inauthentic."

If you were to ask what the limits of the Sudan are, I would say that I have not found anyone who has attempted to define its beginning and end, but Walī al-Dīn Ibn Khaldūn said in his great history, in the account of the kings of the Sudan

25. Al-Kuntī's statement ends here.

neighboring the Maghrib: "Among the Sudanese nations are the Tājira, next to them are the Kanem; to the West of these are the Kawkaw and after them come the Takrūr." He also said in the fourth volume, when writing about the nations of the Sudan, "And the Ethiopians are the greatest nation of the Sudan."

What we have been discussing since the beginning of this chapter with regard to the fact that migration from the lands of the unbelievers is obligatory for all Muslims, cannot be disputed and nobody is excused for neglecting it except the weak. God has said: "Except for the oppressed among the men, women, and children who are unable to devise a plan and are not shown a way,"[26] i.e. who have neither the power nor the funds to migrate, "and are not shown a way" i.e., a way towards a land into which they can migrate, as al-Suyūṭī said in his *Takmila.* In his commentary, explaining the meaning of His words "are unable to devise a plan," al-Khāzin said: "It means those who are incapable of devising a plan, and who have neither the means nor the power to migrate." Concerning such people, God has said: "As for these, it may be that God will pardon them."[27] The commentators said that the expression indicating hope [i.e. "it may be"] and that indicating pardon were mentioned to warn people that failure to migrate is so grave a matter that even a man in difficult circumstances ought not to feel at ease and should be on the lookout for [a way of obeying] the divine precept and set his heart upon it.

O brethren, it is incumbent on you to migrate from the lands of unbelief to the lands of Islam that you may attain Paradise and be companions of your ancestor Abraham, and your Prophet Muḥammad, on account of the Prophet's saying, "Whoever flees with his religion from one land to another, be it [merely the distance of] the span of a hand, will attain Paradise and be the companion of Abraham and the Prophet Muḥammad."

26. Qur'ān 4: 98.
27. Qur'ān 4: 99.

Interpretations of Ibn Fūdī in the Age of British Imperialism in Hausaland

With the establishment of a British protectorate in Hausaland in 1901, many jurists considered it necessary to again address the issue of whether Muslims could live under non-Muslim rule.[28] Qāḍī ʿAbdallāh Ibn ʿAlī's *Epistle and Advice to Contemporaries Who are Concerned with What Will Admit Them to the Community of Saved Muslims* is an attempt to address this question by adapting Ibn Fūdī's and al-Wansharīsī's ideas to the exigencies of the colonial era.[29] The obligation of migration (*hijra*) is the central motif of Ibn ʿAlī's treatise. It is considered a virtue in itself and must be engaged in regardless of its consequences for the believer. Migration, he says, is obligatory from a society ruled by non-Muslims, even if there is neither a community nor a Muslim leader to which the migrant can run:

> Consider his [the Prophet's] words: "Keep away from all those sects even if it means that you gnaw the root of a tree until death overcomes you."[30] Know that *hijra* is not tied to the existence of an [established] Islamic community such that the absence of an Islamic community or Islamic land to which *hijra* could be made would serve as an excuse to abrogate it [*hijra*]... if he emigrates to a place where it is possible for him to practice his religion, doing so even if he is alone in an uninhabited land, he is a Sunnī and the place in which he resides is a Sunnī place.[31]

The dichotomy that Ibn ʿAlī repeatedly draws is between the material world and the life required by Islam. To remain in a non-

28. On the response of the Nigerian jurists to these events, see Muḥammad Umar, *Islam and Colonialism: Intellectual Responses of Muslims of Northern Nigeria to British Rule* (Leiden: Brill, 2006), 68 ff. and R. A. Adeleye, "The Dilemma of the Wazir: The Place of the *Risālat al-wazīr ilā ahl al-ʿilm wa al-tadabbur* in the History of the Conquest of the Sokoto Caliphate," *Journal of the Historical Society of Nigeria* 4 (1968), 285 ff.

29. Muḥammad Umar, *Islam and Colonialism*, 68 ff.

30. Al-Bukhārī, no. 6673.

31. Qāḍī ʿAbdallāh, *Risāla ilā al-muʿāṣirīn*, ed. Omar Bello (Sokoto: The Islamic Academy, n.d), 7a. Cf. 3b-4a.

Muslim society, whether because of concern for wealth or because of concern for one's family, is to shun Islam for the material world. In Ibn ʿAlī's treatise, Ibn Fūdī's concern with the problems of religious syncretism are replaced with a concern about the corrosive effects of Christian culture. He says that when unbelievers interfere in Muslim affairs, they cause Muslims to acquire their

> vile character and reprehensible customs and emulate their forbidden way of life until the weak of heart become accustomed to their shameful customs and the youth are raised in their religion. Women and children are tempted to dress in their garb and to adorn themselves with their finery until... the *Sunna* dies, and iniquitous innovation (*bidʿa*) thrives and their religion is victorious and prevails, and Muslims are humiliated by coming under the rule of the Christians.[32]

Thus, for Ibn ʿAlī, the fundamental form of relations between Muslims and non-Muslims must be limited to *jihād*. A temporary cessation of these hostilities by truce is only possible when instituted for the purpose of allowing Muslims trapped in non-Muslim territory to migrate.[33] Even in the event that the British possess such superior weapons that they stand to annihilate the Muslim community, a truce is not permissible because a truce with the British would destroy Islam so thoroughly that even "its smell would not survive as we see in many lands which they have conquered and imposed conditions which destroy religion, piece by piece, without end."[34] British rule over Muslims cannot be tolerated because it necessitates the abandonment of *jihād*, which is prohibited. It also involves such prohibited activities as the promotion of the Christian religion, the abandonment of commanding right and forbidding wrong,[35] as well as granting non-Muslims

32. Ibid., 5a.
33. Ibid., 4b.
34. Ibid., 5a.
35. The duty of correcting Muslims who transgress is ordained by the Qur'ān. On this duty, see Michael Cook, *Commanding Right and Forbidding Wrong* (Cambridge: Cambridge University Press, 2001), 362.

access to mosques and schools.[36] Any truce containing such provisions is considered unlawful.

Other authorities reject Ibn ʿAlī's uncompromising view on migration from lands ruled by non-Muslims. Muḥammad b. Aḥmad al-Bukhārī (d. 1910), the *wazīr* of Sokoto who officially surrendered the region to the British, accepts the validity of the obligation of migration, but says that it is temporarily inapplicable to the Muslims of Sokoto. Migration, he says, is not required for them because there is "no way of migrating from this land owing to the scarcity of water along the roads or the total lack of it along some of them as well as the severity of heat and the presence of the Christians camped along all the routes."[37] He further attempts to more closely define what the Qurʾān means when it prohibits alliance with the unbelievers. He says that there are three kinds of alliance. The first is that which is motivated by a love for the unbelievers. This kind of alliance is a form of unbelief (*kufr*) and if a person does not repent for participating in it, he is to be executed. The second type is motivated by a desire for material gain. This is understood to be a sin, but it is not unbelief. Finally, there is that alliance which is motivated by fear of the unbeliever. This final kind al-Bukhārī declares to be lawful provided that it is not accompanied by any love for the unbeliever. He classifies this as religiously sanctioned dissimulation (*taqiyya*) and says that it is enjoined by the Qurʾān under such circumstances.[38] This view is supported by Aḥmad b. Saʿd, the *qāḍī* of Gwandu, who emphasizes that, despite British rule, Sokoto is to be classified as a land of belief. He says that British rule does not automatically make Sokoto an abode of war because the British involve themselves only in worldly, but not religious, matters. He adds, however, that were all Muslims to leave Sokoto, the land would indeed revert to being one of unbelief.[39] In view of this undesirable consequence, he rejects the option of migration from Sokoto.

36. Ibid., 5b.
37. Adeleye, "The Dilemma of the Wazir," Arabic: 299, English: 306.
38. Ibid., Arabic: 300-301, English: 306-307.
39. Ibid., Arabic: 302, English: 309.

Thus, in the face of the overwhelming power of the British, the Nigerian scholars (*ʿulamāʾ*) attempted to redefine the significance of Ibn Fūdī's teachings on migration. The validity of migration from the abode of war as a religious precept was not challenged, but the exigencies of maintaining a religious community forced its neglect, even if this neglect was regarded as only temporary.

– 3 –

India

When a land is not safe for Islam a Muslim has only two alternatives, Jehad or Hijrat.[1] *That is to say, he must either make use of every force God has given him for the liberation of the land and the ensurement of perfect freedom for the practice and preaching of Islam, or he must migrate to some other and freer land with a view to return[ing] to it when it is once more safe for Islam. ... In view of our weak condition, migration is the only alternative for us. ... This step, which we shall now have to consider with all the seriousness that its very nature demands, will be perhaps the most decisive in the history of our community since the Hijrat of our Holy Prophet.*[2]

Beginning in the mid-seventeenth century, the British East India Company assumed rule over vast parts of India. The British arrival, however, does not seem to have provoked much of a response from the Muslim scholars in this early period. It has been suggested that this was because the East India Company did not extensively interfere in the affairs of the Islamic law courts.[3] It is also possible that it was because the phenomenon of non-Muslim rule was already well-known in India prior to the arrival of the British and there was an established protocol of how to deal with it. An exam-

1. I have not modified the author's transliterations of Arabic in this section. In this case, *jehad* and *hijrat* would normally be rendered *jihād* and *hijra*. Also, where Indian authors bear Arabic names, I have rendered them in the manner that they usually appear and without diacritics.

2. M. Naeem Qureshi, "The ʿUlamāʾ of British India and the Hijrat of 1920," *Modern Asian Studies* 13 (1979), 43.

3. Peter Hardy, *The Muslims of British India* (London: Cambridge University Press, 1972), 50 ff.

ple of this protocol is found in the work of the prominent, eighteenth-century Indian scholar, Muḥammad Aʿlā b. Shaykh ʿAlī al-Tahānawī.[4] Al-Tahānawī quotes an unnamed authority describing how Muslims should conduct life under the Hindu Marathas:

> [Regarding] a Muslim land which is under the rule of unbelievers who permit Muslims to conduct the Friday and festival prayers, and appoint judges (*qāḍīs*) who satisfy the Muslims, but in which the Muslims must let them appoint a Muslim governor for them... this calamity has occurred in our time with the rule of the unbelievers over some of our abodes and it is necessary to know the laws [which apply to this situation]. The truth is that, without a doubt, the Muslim lands which are in their hands [have the status of] the "abode of Islam." This is because they are not bordered by their lands and because they do not manifest their laws in it.[5] Rather, the Muslim judges and officials render judgment according to the laws of the Islamic religion. As for when they [the Muslims] refer their cases to the scholars (*ʿulamāʾ*) of this [unbelieving] community and are judged by them, a Muslim who complies with and obeys them out of necessity acts in accordance with Islam, and praise God for that, but if he obeys them not out of necessity... [he is among] the sinful, but not the apostates. To call [such people] apostates is the greatest of sins.[6]

According to this text, it was not necessary to label areas controlled by the Marathas as abodes of war, with all of the destabilizing consequences that that entailed. Provided that Muslims retained control over legal matters, it was of no consequence that they were governed from above by an appointee of the unbelievers. Thus the fact that Muslim scholars provided no response in the early stages of East India Company rule could have been because they envisaged it as continuing the policy of the Marathas. It was only in the

4. Neither the birth nor death date of this scholar is known. His major work, however, was finished in 1158/1745. See *E.I.*^{2}, s.v. "al-Tahānawī."

5. On these criteria, see Khadduri, *War and Peace in the Law of Islam*, 156.

6. Muḥammad Aʿlā b. ʿAlī al-Tahānawī, *Aḥkām al-arāḍī*, ed. ʿAbdallāh al-Ṭurayqī (Riyadh: n.p., 2001), 70-71.

late eighteenth century, when the Company instituted laws which infringed upon Islamic control of legal matters, that Muslim scholars began to think that a revision of their previous position was warranted.[7]

The most prominent scholar to develop this new position was Shāh ʿAbd al-ʿAzīz (d. 1239/1823), a Delhi scholar and the son of one of the greatest figures in Indian Islam, Shāh Walī Allāh (d. 1176/1762). Some of ʿAbd al-ʿAzīz's disciples paint him as the architect of resistance to the British. They credit him with being the first to label British India an abode of war and to demand migration from it. An analysis of ʿAbd al-ʿAzīz's fatwās, however, presents a different picture.[8] ʿAbd al-ʿAzīz did indeed declare British India to be an abode of war.[9] His reasoning for this appears in one of his fatwās:

> In this city [Delhi] the Muslim leader holds no authority while the decrees of the Christian leaders are obeyed... Promulgation of the commands of unbelief means that in matters of administration, control of the people, levying land-tax, tribute, tolls and customs, the punishment of thieves and robbers, and the settlement of disputes..., the unbelievers act according to their discretion. There are, it is true, certain Islamic rituals, e.g., the Friday and ʿĪd prayers, the call to prayer and cow-slaughter, with which they do not interfere – but that is of no account. The basic principles of these rituals are of no value to them, because they demolish mosques without the least hesitation.[10]

However, despite declaring British India to be an abode of war, ʿAbd al-ʿAzīz does not encourage Muslims to launch a *jihād*, as classical jurisprudence would have mandated for such territories.

7. Hardy, *The Muslims of British India*, 31 ff.

8. Barbara Metcalf, *Islamic Revival in British India*, 50 ff. Cf. Ziya-ul-Hasan Faruqi, *The Deoband School and the Demand for Pakistan* (New York: Asia Publishing House, 1963), 2.

9. Mushirul Haq, *Shah Abdul ʿAziz: His Life and Time* (Lahore: Institute of Islamic Culture, 1996), 51 and 42.

10. M. Mujeeb, *The Indian Muslims* (Montreal: McGill University Press, 1967), 390-91.

Instead, he allows Muslims to do such things as learn English, eat with Christians (provided that the food is lawful)[11] and accept employment from Christians, even governmental employment, providing that this employment does not entail fighting Muslims. At one point, he indicates with regret that the activities which he had permitted have led some Muslims to become "well-wishers" of the Christians with whom they interact. This realization, however, does not lead him to significantly revise his previous position. He confirms that employment with Christians is lawful, but says that recipients of this employment should take care that it "is of the kind in which men do not become very close with the unbelievers."[12] He is thus clear that while territories controlled by the British must be branded abodes of war, this abode of war is not one that is categorized by violence. In particular, ʿAbd al-ʿAzīz does not require Muslims who live in such territory to migrate or wage *jihād*. Muslims should only migrate, he says, from those countries where the unbelievers prohibit them from practicing Islamic rites, such as fasting, prayer and circumcision. If Muslims are practicing all of these rights in public, migration is not obligatory."[13] He thus permits Muslims to remain and to live normal lives in British India.

However, despite the fact that ʿAbd al-ʿAzīz's designation of British India as the abode of war was not accompanied by a philosophy of active resistance to the British, it could be argued that it paved the way for his disciples to articulate such a position. Thus, for example, Sayyid Aḥmad, a disciple of ʿAbd al-ʿAzīz and the founder of a prominent movement against the British, considered India to be an abode of war and consequently migrated from it.[14] He wrote:

> While in India I thought of a place of peace where I could take Muslims and organize *jihād*. In spite of its extent of hundreds of miles, I could not find a place to which I could mi-

11. Ibid., 49.
12. Ibid., 45.
13. Quoted in Mushirul Haq, *Shah Abdul ʿAziz*, 51.
14. Mujeeb, *The Indian Muslims*, 395.

> grate. There were many who advised me to carry on *jihād* in India, promising to provide me with whatever was necessary by way of material, treasure and weapons. But I could not agree to this, for *jihād* must be in accordance with the *sunna*. Mere rebellion was not intended.[15]

The idea that migration from British territory was required of all Muslims under British rule in India was vividly expounded in a pamphlet by an anonymous author, the original of which is no longer extant, but which was translated by a British official. There is no date on the pamphlet, but the official's translation was published in 1870 and he indicates that it was in circulation at that time.

Anonymous: Treatise on Migration
(c. 1870)[16]

In the name of God, the merciful and kind God is all goodness. He is the Lord of the Universe. May divine kindness and safety attend Muhammad, His messenger, and all his descendants and companions. Now you should know that it is incumbent on all Muhammadans[17] to leave a country which is governed by an unbeliever, in which acting according to the Muhammadan law is forbidden by the ruling power. If they do not abandon it, then in the hour of death

15. Sayyid Ahmad Shahid, quoted in Mujeeb, *The Indian Muslims*, 395.
16. From "The Wahhabis in India," *Calcutta Review* 51 (October 1870), 388-89. I have slightly modified the translation for stylistic reasons.
17. I.e., Muslims. In the English usage of the nineteenth century, the terms Muhammadan and Musalman were used interchangeably to translate the Arabic word "Muslim." At this time, such usage did not necessarily reflect either anti-Muslim sentiment or ignorance of Muslim self-understanding. Indeed, particularly in India, some Muslims themselves used these terms in order to self-identify. Nowadays, it is considered improper to use the term Muhammadan as many Muslims understand it to imply that they are worshippers of Muḥammad rather than worshippers of God. On this, see Irshad Abdal-Haqq, "Islamic Law: An Overview of Its Origin and Elements," in *Understanding Islamic Law*, ed. Hisham Ramadan (Lanham: Rowman and Littlefield, 2006), 8 and Annemarie Schimmel, *And Muhammad is His Messenger* (Chapell Hill: University of North Carolina Press, 1985), 217 ff.

when their souls will be separated from their bodies, they will suffer great torments. When the angel of death will come to separate their souls from their bodies, he will ask them the following question: Was not the kingdom of God sufficiently spacious to enable you to leave your homes and settle in another country? And saying this he will subject them to great pain in separating their souls from their bodies. Afterwards they will suffer the torments of the grave without intermission, and on the Day of Judgment they will be cast into hell, where they will suffer eternal punishment. May God forbid that Muhammadans should die in a country ruled over by an unbeliever. If he dies in such a country his sufferings at the time of death will be great; afterwards he will undergo the torment of the grave, and his punishment on the Day of Judgment is beyond comprehension. O Brethren! death has not yet come. Make your escape now. Go to a country which is governed by Musalmans and live there in the land of the faithful. If you reach it alive, then all the sins you may have committed during your life time will be forgiven. Do not trouble yourself about the means of livelihood, God, who provides for all, will give you your food wherever you may be. Up to the present God has not suffered any person to live in a state of starvation and nakedness. As for you, you are leaving your homes by Divine command, and the Lord has promised you in the Quran, great opportunities, advancement, and Divine favor. What do you fear? The Ruler of Heaven and Earth is always with you; you will find means of obtaining your daily food in the land you are going to. Do not give it a thought. Go and follow there the trade or profession which you follow here. God provides for all. Let your heart be at ease. He will give you the means of blessing your daily bread in a respectable manner wherever you go. And all your sins will be forgiven. You will live comfortably in this life and the angel of death will separate your soul from your body without causing pain. For you the grave will have no torment, the Day of Judgment no terror, and you will be saved from the pains of Hell.

It is related in the traditions[18] that there was once an Israelite who murdered ninety-nine men unjustly, and afterwards, going to a holy man confessed his crimes, and asked him how he could obtain forgiveness. The holy man answered as follows: "If any person unjustly kills even one man, he will certainly be damned. Your sins will not be forgiven. You will certainly go to Hell." And hearing this the Israelite said: "I must go to Hell, that is certain. I shall therefore kill you in order to make up a hundred murders." He then killed the holy man, and going to another holy man confessed that he had committed one hundred murders and asked him how he could obtain forgiveness. And he was answered, by sincere repentance and the performance of *hijra*. As soon as he heard this he repented of his sins and leaving his country set out for a foreign land. On the way death approached and both the angels, viz. the angel of mercy and the angel of punishment, appeared to separate his soul from his body. The angel of mercy said that he would separate the man's soul from his body because he had repented of his sins and performed *hijra;* and the angel of punishment admitted that if he had succeeded in reaching another kingdom the duty of causing the separation would have been partly the right of the angel of mercy; but declared his intention of performing the operation and subjecting the man to great torments (because he was still within his own kingdom) and had not succeeded in completing the *hijra*. Then both angels measured the land on which the man was lying, and found that one of his feet had crossed the boundary and lay within another kingdom, and the angel of mercy, declaring that his right was established, painlessly separated the man's soul from his body, and he (the man) was admitted amongst those favored by God. You have heard how *hijra* is rewarded in the next world. So let you all pray to God for grace to enable you to

18. This tradition is discussed in Robert Hoyland, "History, Fiction and Authorship in the First Centuries of Islam," in *Writing and Representation in Medieval Islam*, ed. Julia Bray (Abingdon: Routledge, 2006), 21.

> perform *hijra*, and perform it quickly, lest you die in an unbelieving country. If you do, you will suffer great afflictions. When death comes repentance is too late. Do now what you wish to do.

Fatwās in Favor of British Rule

The British were concerned about developments in Islamic thought which might encourage migration from British territory and resistance. In order to ward off a rebellion by the Muslims of India, they went to considerable lengths to obtain fatwās from Islamic scholars which forbade it. Some of these efforts were detailed in a report requested by the viceroy of India, Lord Mayo,[19] entitled, "The Indian Musalmans: Are They Bound in Conscience to Rebel against the Queen."[20] British efforts at obtaining fatwās met with considerable success. One British official, William Hunter, remarked that "during the past few years a whole phalanx of fatwas or authoritative decisions have appeared on this side and even the three great high priests at Mecca have been enlisted to liberate the Indian Musulmans from the dangerous duty of rebellion against the English crown."[21] As a result, he says that, for Muslims, "the duty of waging war has… disappeared":

> The present generation of Musalmans are bound, according to their own texts, to accept the *status quo*. They are not responsible for it, and they are forbidden, in the face of God's providence, and with regard to the immense perils in which a revolt would involve the True Faith, to have recourse to arms. They are compelled to adhere to the mutual relation which has sprung up between the rulers and the ruled, and to perform their duties as subjects so long as we maintain their status (*amán*) sufficiently intact to enable them to discharge the duties of their religion.[22]

---

19. I.e., Richard Southwell Bourke, 6th Earl of Mayo (d. 1872).
20. Interestingly, subsequent editions of the work omit its subtitle.
21. W. W. Hunter, *The Indian Musalmans*, 3rd edition (London: Trübner and Co., 1876), 114.
22. Ibid., 140.

However, despite this, Hunter is still skeptical of the loyalty of the Muslims of India. He says that "the [Islamic] Law and the Prophets can be utilized on the side of loyalty as well as on the side of corruption"[23] and adds that "it is hopeless to look for anything like enthusiastic loyalty from our Muhammadan subjects. But we can reasonably expect that so long as we scrupulously discharge our obligations to them, they will honestly fulfill their duties in the position in which God has placed them to us."[24]

Below are fatwās, hailing from both India and Mecca, which the British received warning Muslims against rebelling and also stating that British India is a part of the abode of Islam. They appear as they were translated in Hunter's appendix as scholars have been unable to trace the originals.[25]

Fatwās from Mecca on British Rule in India[26]
(late-nineteenth century)

[Question]

What is your opinion (may your greatness continue forever) on this question; whether the country of Hindustan, the rulers of which are Christians, and who do not interfere with all the injunctions of Islam such as the ordinary daily prayers, the prayers of the two 'Ids, etc., but do authorize departure from a few of the injunctions of Islam, such as the permission to inherit the property of the Muhammadan ancestor to one who changes his religion (being that of his ancestors), and becomes a Christian, is Dar-ul-Islam or not? Answer the above, for which God will reward you.

23. Ibid., 122.

24. Ibid., 141.

25. As a result of this, an Arabic work which dealt with the British in India was actually forced to translate parts of the fatwās back into Arabic from these English versions. See Khādim Ḥusayn Ilāhī Bakhsh, *Athar al-fikr al-Gharbī fī inḥirāf al-mujtama' al-Muslim bi-shibh al-qārra al-Hindiyya* (Mecca: Dār Ḥarrā', 1988).

26. Hunter, *The Indian Musalmans*, 3rd edition (London: Trübner and Co., 1876), 217-19.

[Answer 1]

All praises are due to the Almighty, who is the Lord of all the creation! O Almighty, increase my knowledge!

As long as even some of the peculiar observances of Islam prevail in it, it is the Dar-ul-Islam.

The Almighty is omniscient, pure and high!

This is the *order* passed by one who hopes for the secret favour of the Almighty, who praises God, and prays for blessings and peace on his Prophet.

Jamāl Ibn ʿAbdallāh [Ibn] Shaykh ʿUmar al-Ḥanafī (d.1284/ 1867),[27]
the present Muftī of Mecca (the Honoured).
May God favour him and his father.

[Answer 2]

All praises are due to God, who is one; and may the blessings of God be showered upon our chief, Muḥammad, and upon his descendants and companions, and upon the followers of his faith!

O God! I require guidance from Thee in righteousness.

Yes! As long as even some of the peculiar observances of Islam prevail in it, it is Dar-ul-Islam.

The Almighty is omniscient, pure and high!

This is written by one who hopes for salvation from the God of mercy. May God forgive him, and his parents and preceptors, and brothers and friends, and all Muhammadans.

Aḥmad Ibn Zaynī Daḥlān [d. 1304/1886],
Muftī of the Shāfiʿī Sect of Mecca (the Protected)

27. Muḥammad Saʿīd b. Muḥammad Bā Baṣīl (d. 1330/1911), see ʿAbdallāh b. ʿAbd al-Raḥmān al-Muʿallimī, *Aʿlām al-Makkīyīn min al-qarn al-tāsiʿ ilā al-qarn al-rābiʿ ʿashar al-hijrī* (Mecca: Muʾassasat al-Furqān liʾl-Turāth al-Islāmī, 2000), 1: 68.

[Answer 3]

All praises are due to God, who is one! O Almighty! Increase my knowledge! It is written in the commentary of Dasoki[28] that a country of Islam does not become Dar-ul-Harb as soon as it passes into the hands of the Infidels, but only when all or most of the injunctions of Islam disappear therefrom.

God is omniscient! May the blessings of God be showered upon our Chief, Muhammad, and on his descendants and companions.

Ḥusayn Ibn Ibrāhīm (d. 1292/1875),[29]
Muftī of the Mālikī Sect of Mecca (the Illustrious)

The Decision of the Law Doctors of Northern India

Translation of the *istifta* or question put by Sayyid Amir Husain, personal assistant to the commissioner of Bhagalpur

[Question]

What is your decision, O men of learning and expounders of the law of Islam in the following: Whether a jihad is lawful in India, a country formerly held by a Muhammadan ruler and now held under the sway of a Christian government, where the said Christian ruler does in no way interfere with his Muhammadan subjects in the rites prescribed by their religion, such as praying, fasting, pilgrimage, *zakat*, Friday prayer and *jama'at*, and gives them fullest protection and liberty in the above respects in the same way as a Muhammadan ruler would do, and where the Muhammadan subjects have no strength and means to fight with their rulers; on the contrary, there is every chance of the war, if waged, ending with a defeat and thereby causing an indignity to Islam.

28. I.e., Muḥammad b. Aḥmad b. ʿArafa al-Dasūqī (d. 1230/1815), *Ḥāshiyat al-Dasūqī ʿalā al-Sharḥ al-kabīr li-Abī al-Barakāt Aḥmad al-Dardīr.*
29. al-Muʿallimī, *Aʿlām al-Makkīyīn*, 2: 826.

Please answer quoting your authority.

[Answer]

The Musalmans here are protected by Christians and there is no jihad in a country where protection is afforded, as the absence of protection and liberty between Musalmans and infidels is essential in a religious war, and that condition does not exist here. Besides it is necessary that there should be a probability of victory to Musalmans and glory to the Indians. If there be no such probability, the jihad is unlawful.

Here the Maulavis quote Arabic passages from *Manhaj-ul-Ghaffar*[30] and the *Fatawi-i-Alamgiri*, supporting the above decision.

Maulavi Ali Muhammad of Lucknow
Maulavi Abd-ul-Hai of Lucknow
Maulavi Fazlullah of Lucknow
Muhammad Naim of Lucknow
Maulavi Rahmatullah of Lucknow
Maulavi Kutab-ud-din of Dehli
Maulavi Lutfullah of Rampur
and others...

17th Rabi'-us-sani or Rabi II, 1287 H.,
corresponding with the 17th July 1870

30. I.e., *Minaḥ al-ghaffār sharḥ tanwīr al-abṣār* by Muḥammad b. ʿAbdallāh al-Khaṭīb al-Tamartāshī (d. 1004/1597).

Karamat ʿAli: British India Is the Abode of Islam

According to Karamat ʿAli (d. 1290/1873),[31] a student of Shāh ʿAbd al-ʿAzīz, and a prolific and widely respected author of works of theology and jurisprudence, not only was rebellion against the British prohibited, but British India was also a part of the abode of Islam.[32] In November of 1870, he was invited by the Mahomedan Literary Society of Calcutta to give a lecture on this topic and a summary of the proceedings of that lecture was published in booklet form. Karamat ʿAli is of the opinion that Islamic law prohibits Muslims from resisting the British. However, he says that the reasons that are often given for this position are wrong because they proceed on the basis that India is an abode of war. As Karamat ʿAli sees it, however, it is better to argue that British India is a part of the abode of Islam and thus preempt all discussion of waging a jihād.

Karamat ʿAli claims that his approach to the problem is consistent with Ḥanafī[33] legal doctrine. According to the Ḥanafīs, he says, there are three different events, any one of which should prompt Muslims to ask whether their land has become a part of the abode of war: (1) when non-Muslims conquer the country, (2) when the Muslim inhabitants of a city convert from Islam and begin enforcing non-Islamic law, and (3) when non-Muslims who have been living as subjects under Muslims gain power and rule over and subjugate Muslims. Once the question has been asked, he introduces three conditions which must be satisfied to bring about a change in the status of a land from the abode of Islam to the abode of war: (1) when non-Muslims rule and Islamic law is not observed, (2) when the abode becomes geographically contiguous with non-

31. See *Encyclopedia of Islam*, 2nd ed., s.v., "Karāmat ʿAlī."

32. *Abstract of the Proceedings of the Mahomedan Literary Society of Calcutta at a Meeting Held at the Residence of Moulvie Abdool Luteef Khan Bahadoor on Wednesday, the 23rd November, 1870. Lecture by Moulvie Karamat Ali (of Jounpore) on a Question of Mahomedan Law Involving the Duty of Mahomedans in British India Towards the Ruling Power* (Calcutta, 1871).

33. The Ḥanafī legal school was the Sunnī school of Islamic law which was dominant in India.

Islamic lands and isolated from Islamic ones, and (3) when Muslims do not enjoy religious liberty and *dhimmīs* become superior to them.

Elaborating on these issues, Karamat ʿAli says that there is both a jurisprudential question and a factual question which must be dealt with. The jurisprudential question is whether *all* of these conditions have to be met simultaneously for the abode's status to change, or whether the status changes if *any* one of these conditions are met. The factual question is whether any or all of these conditions have been met in the case of British India.

The answer to the jurisprudential question hinges on whether a polity loses its status as the abode of Islam in the same way that it gains it – through conquest or conversion – or whether it loses its status only when everything which now makes it Islamic is removed. The answer to the factual question, according to Karamat ʿAli, lies not in whether Muslims hold ultimate political power, but rather in whether their laws and culture are in force. Moreover, it is less important that non-Muslims (in the form of the British) have become politically superior than it is that those non-Muslims who were *dhimmīs* and the inferiors of Muslim (i.e., the Hindus), have not experienced a role-reversal.

Booklet Containing a Lecture of Karamat ʿAli on "a Question of Mahomedan Law Involving the Duty of Mahomedans in British India Towards the Ruling Power"[34]
(1870)

It has been suggested by gentlemen whose opinions are entitled to respect, that some explanation is necessary why the proceedings were held, which are recorded in the following

34. *Abstract of the Proceedings of the Mahomedan Literary Society of Calcutta at a Meeting Held at the Residence of Moulvie Abdool Luteef Khan Bahadoor on Wednesday, the 23rd November, 1870. Lecture by Moulvie Karamat Ali (of Jounpore) on a Question of Mahomedan Law Involving the Duty of Mahomedans in British India Towards the Ruling Power* (Calcutta, 1871).

pages. This is easily supplied. Some time ago, a letter appeared in the English newspapers signed by a Mahomedan officer of government employed at Bhagulpore, in which he congratulated himself and the public on having made the discovery that the followers of Islam are not bound by their religion to rebel against the British government. The same announcement was made through all the Oordoo newspapers in the country. It was indeed as if the Mahomedan world were ignorant of the fact before; and that Mahomedans, who had in blindness been hatching treason and rebellion against their beneficent rulers, were to refrain hereafter on being blessed with this new flood of light!

Such inferences from the publication of the *fatwah* from Lucknow and Delhi, by the officer alluded to were unavoidable; and great was the surprise and indignation of a large number of Mahomedan gentlemen in this city, who knew better. It was felt by them to be imperative that a public exposition of Mahomedan law should be held, in which it should be proclaimed, that such a question as that which elicited the *fatwah* was not one which a good Mahomedan in British India should for a moment entertain. The visit of Moulvie Karamat Ali to Calcutta seemed a favourable opportunity for the purpose; and the proceedings are the result.

Abstract Translation of the Proceedings, in Oordoo, of the Sixth Monthly Meeting of the Mahomedan Literary Society of Calcutta, (Eighth Year), held at the house of the Secretary, Moulvie Abdool Luteef Khan Bahadoor, at No- 16 Toltollah, on the 23rd of November 1870, at 8 pm.

A very large number of Mahomedan gentlemen were present. Kazee[35] Abdool Baree, president, in the chair.

After the usual preliminary business of the society was over, the secretary introduced to the meeting, Moulvie Karamat Ali of Jounpore, well known as a successful preacher of

35. I.e., *qāḍī* or judge.

the Hanafee sect of the Sunnee Mahomedans, who had spent 50 years of his life in following the vocation of a public preacher in Bengal, chiefly in the eastern districts. He, the secretary said, had undertaken to deliver a lecture, in which he would maintain the following thesis on the principles of Mahomedan law:—"That, according to Mahomedan law, British India is *Darul Islam*, and that it is not lawful for the Mahomedans of British India to make jihad."

The Moulvie then delivered a discourse, of which the following is a summary.

He said that, during his present sojourn in Calcutta, he had been asked the two following questions of law and religion, by certain ignorant Mahomedans.

1st. — Whether, according to the religious tenets of the Hanafee Sect, British India is *Darul Islam* (country of Islam or safety) or *Darul Harb* (country of war or enmity).

2nd. — Whether it is lawful or not for the Mahomedans of British India to wage war against their rulers who profess the Christian religion.

At first, he was surprised to hear such questions, and could not understand why they should be asked this year? He had come to Calcutta before, but was never similarly questioned; but the mystery became clear on his learning that a certain *fatwah* (opinion of the doctors of Mahomedan law) had been published in the Oordoo newspapers, and it had stirred people's minds to make the inquiries he mentioned. At first, it occurred to him that a dissertation might be written on the questions, (which in fact tend to one and the same issue); and it might be published in order that such doubts as might arise in the minds of men might be removed; and also that he might be spared the trouble of replying to everyone individually. Meanwhile, he had an interview with Moulvie Abdool Luteef Khan Bahadoor, secretary to this society; and, in the course of conversation, the secretary said, that, if the dissertation were read at a meeting of this society, the object of publicity would be fully attained; while, under the by-laws of the

Society, the dissertation might be printed and published by the Society itself. He also said, that the president of the Society was the acknowledged head of the learned Mahomedans of this city; and amongst the members too, there were many learned men. Now, if these gentlemen approved of the dissertation, its conclusions would be placed beyond doubt or cavil. He, the speaker, highly approved of this suggestion; and promised that, if he got a few days' previous notice of any meeting of this Society, he would attend it, and read out his dissertation before the meeting. Accordingly, he had information of this meeting. But, having had urgent engagements on hand, he had been unable to get the dissertation ready; instead therefore of a written discourse, he would state verbally what he had intended to embody in the paper; and, if the same be approved by those present, it could be reduced to writing; and the members of the Society would then be able to give it publicity in any way that pleased them.

But to come to the point:— British India, which is at present under a Christian government, is *Darul Islam* (country of Islam or safety), according to the dogmas of the Hanafee sect. Such is the *fatwah* (opinion of the doctors of Mahomedan law). For such is the assertion of the celebrated lawgiver Imam Aboo Haneefah; and the same has been laid down, either expressly or by implication, in all treatises of Mahomedan law current in India; such as the *Hidayah*, *Sharhi-Vikayah*, *Jami ur-Rumooz*, *Durrul- Mukhtar* and its two Commentaries, the *Tahtavee*, and the *Raddul-Muhtar*; *Fatawa Alamgeeree*, *Fatawa Kozee Khan*, *Bahrur Raik*, *Nahrul Faik*, *Fusool Imadee*, *Nihayatul Murad*, *Ibrahim-Shahee* , *Ashbah-Wan-Nazair*, &c. As however it would tax the patience of the meeting to be obliged to listen to a recital of passages from all these books, all to the same purport, he would read passages only from the *Fatawa Alamgeeree* and *Fusool Imadee*, which contain the opinions of the learned doctors of both earlier and later times, and are considered the most reliable authorities. In the *Fatawa Alamgeeree*, it is said:—

Know ye, that the existence of only one condition is sufficient to convert *Darul Harb* into *Darul Islam*; and that condition is, that the rule of Islam become established in *Darul Harb*. Imam Mahomed (the second disciple of Imam Aboo Haneefah, the head of the doctors of Mahomedan law, according to the Sunnees, and the founder of the Hanafee sect) has said in a work, called the *Zyadat*, that, according to Imam Aboo Haneefah, a country which was *Darul Islam* does not become *Darul Harb* except on the three following conditions being co-existent in it: —

1st. That the rule of infidels is openly exercised, and the ordinances of Islam are not observed.

2nd. That it is in such contiguity to a country which is *Darul Harb*, that no city of *Darul Islam* intervenes between that country and *Darul Harb*.

3rd. That no Moslem is found in the enjoyment of religious liberty, nor a *zimmee* (an infidel who has accepted the terms of permanent subjection to Moslem rule), under the same terms as he enjoyed under the Government of Islam.

There are three different occasions, on which this question may arise; namely, 1st, when the inhabitants of *Darul Harb* conquer any country belonging to Moslems; 2ndly, when the inhabitants of a city turn apostates and enforce the observance of the principles of infidels; 3rdly, when *zimmee*s violate the conditions on which they live under a contract of subjection to Mahomedans, and obtain supremacy in their own country. Such a country does not become *Darul Harb* on the occurrence of any one of these events; but on the existence simultaneously of all the three conditions stated above. Imams Aboo Yusaff and Mahomed, the two disciples of Imam Aboo Haneefah, have however held that the existence of only one condition is sufficient to convert *Darul Islam* into *Darul Harb*, namely — the open establishment in it of the rule of infidels. But they have formed this opinion on principles of simple analogy; that is to say, as *Darul Harb* becomes *Darul Islam* simply by the establishment of the Moslem power in it; so those learned commentators have held that *Darul Harb* becomes *Darul Islam* merely on the existence of one condition, viz:—the establishment of the rule of Islam in it. Therefore, they have drawn the analogy that *Darul Islam* too becomes *Darul Harb* on the existence of but one condition, namely, the establishment of the rule of the infidels in it. Thus, when a *Darul Islam* becomes *Darul Harb* on the occurrence of all the above-mentioned three conditions—.[36]

The author of the *Durrul Mukhtar* has laid down the following general principle in his works:—

The most accurate procedure is that mentioned in the *Sirajia* and other law books; viz., that the final decision should be given in all cases in accordance with the opinion of the chief imam (Aboo Haneefah). But, if his opinion be not forthcoming with reference to any point, then that point should be decided in accordance with the opinion of the second imam, (Aboo Yusaff, first disciple of Imam Aboo Haneefah). Again, when his (the second imam's) opinion is not forthcoming on any point, it would then be decided in accordance with the opinion of the third imam, (Imam Mahomed, second disciple of Imam Aboo Haneefah). When, however, no opinion of even Imam Mahomed be forthcoming on any point, in such a case the decisions should be given according to the opinion of Imams Zafar and Hasan Ibn Zyad.

Following this general principle the question now before the meeting should be decided according to the opinion of the chief imam, Aboo Haneefah. Moreover, the compilers of the *Fatawa Alamgeeree* a body of the most learned Mahomedans of their time, have agreed in holding the same opinion on this question with the chief imam, as is clear from the last mentioned passage of the above-mentioned quotation, namely,

36. The last sentence of this paragraph is difficult to understand and might have been erroneously inserted.

that when "*Darul Islam* becomes *Darul Harb* on the occurrence of all the three above-mentioned conditions..." For if they did not think that the question should be decided according to the opinion of the chief imam — how could they deduce the doctrine that *Darul Islam* becomes *Darul Harb* on the occurrence of all the three above mentioned conditions?

The learned lecturer, before quoting from the *Fusool Imadee*, said, that, as the first part of the passage of *Fusool Imadee* on this subject exactly tallied in style and spirit with the passage quoted from the *Fatawa Alamgeeree*, he would merely recite the latter part of that passage in which the reasons of the chief imam are given as to why *Darul Islam* is not converted into *Darul Harb*, except on all the three said conditions being present simultaneously:—

"This city (viz., the one under consideration) has at first become *Darul Islam* on account of the rule of Islam having been established in it. Now, so long as even some of the ordinances of Islam remain in force there, the city will continue to be *Darul Islam* according to the well-known maxim (of the principles of Mahomedan law), that, whenever a decision is arrived at on account of a certain cause, that decision would continue in force, so long as even a portion of the said cause continues. This text has been quoted from the commentary by Shaikhul Islam Aboo Bakar on the standard work *Seir-ul-Asl*."

After reciting these passages, the learned Moulvie called upon the meeting to consider that not a single one of the three conditions mentioned is to be found in this country. The first does not exist here. For, although the government of Christian rulers prevails, still most of the injunctions of Islam are in force among the Mahomedans. The injunctions of Islam that have reference to worship and prayer are in force here entirely. There is no hindrance whatever to their observance. The injunctions of Islam, that have reference to secular duties are also mostly in full force, in question of marriage, divorce, dower, maintenance, inheritance, gift, endowment, pre-emption, will, and the like, arising amongst Mahomedans. The Mahomedan law is strictly acted upon. It is in exact accordance with the rules laid down in the Mahomedan law, that these questions between parties professing the Mahomedan religion are decided by the judicial officers, be they Christians or Hindoos. And, especially in questions relating to preemption, the injunctions of Islam are in force even amongst the Hindoos up to the present day.

The second condition too does not exist in this country. For, not to speak of the countries beyond the frontiers of India, there are many small principalities in the very heart of the country which can be undoubtedly termed *Darul Islam*. And, as for the countries beyond the western and northwestern frontiers of this country, they are all nothing but *Darul Islam*.

As to the non-existence of the third condition in this country, it is so clear that no argument whatever is necessary. On the contrary, it is a Christian nation that has come to this country from *Darul Harb*; and God has given that nation supremacy in this country, and it has become the ruling power. Now, the entire Mahomedan population of this country, amounting to more than a third of the inhabitants, have continued just as they were before the advent of the British, and the remaining two-thirds are Hindoos, who were *zimmee*s, (or living under a contract of permanent subjection) during the Mahomedan sway, and are in no wise worse off. The population of this country consists almost entirely of these two nations. The Christians, though the ruling nation, are very few in number, and probably less numerous than their co-religionists in other countries, ruled over by Mahomedan kings — such as Turkey and Persia.

The worthy speaker then said that, it having been clearly demonstrated that British India is *Darul Islam*, the doubt that might arise in the minds of some of the ignorant classes of Mahomedans, whether it is incumbent on Mahomedans to make *hijrat* (or emigrate from this country) or not, is also removed. For flight is incumbent on a Mahomedan from *Darul Harb* and not from this country which is *Darul Islam*. If it be incumbent to fly from this country, then it would likewise be incumbent to fly from Turkey and Egypt.

The second question is, "Whether it is lawful in this country to make jihad or not." This has been solved together with the first. For jihad can by no means be lawfully made in *Darul Islam*. This is so evident that it requires no argument or authority to support it. Now, if any misguided wretch, owing to his perverse fortune, were to wage war against the ruling powers of this country, British India, such war would be rightly pronounced rebellion; and rebellion is strictly forbidden by the Mahomedan law. Therefore such war will likewise be unlawful; and in case anyone would wage such war, the Mahomedan subjects would be bound to assist their rulers; and, in conjunction with their rulers, to fight with such rebels. The above has been clearly laid down in the *Fatawa Alamgeeree*.

On the conclusion of the above discourse, Moulvie Fozli Ali, with the permission of the president, read a paper in Persian in support of the lecture.

In the beginning of the paper the same passages from works on Mahomedan law that were quoted by Moulvie Karamat Ali, were alluded to as also others of equal force. At the end, however, Moulvie Fazli Ali said, that, if this country be pronounced *Darul Harb*, (according to the tenets of the Wahabees[37]), and not *Darul Islam*, it would then be unlawful for Mahomedans to live here permanently; and hence it would be imperative upon them to make *hijrat* (or depart from this country). But the fact is, that, since the commence-

37. This is a notoriously slippery term which was employed both by British and Indian Muslims to designate those who were in favor of waging *jihād*. For a history of its use, see Marcia Hermansen, "Fakirs, Wahhabis and Others: Reciprocal Classifications and the Transformation of Intellectual Categories," in *Perspectives of Mutual Encounters in South Asian History, 1760-1860*, ed. Jamal Malik (Leiden: Brill, 2000), 30 ff.

ment of the British rule in this country, upwards of a hundred years ago, thousands and thousands of the most learned, holy, and pious Mahomedans have been born, and have lived here all their lives. And, although they had the ability, yet they did not fly away from this country, but died here. Nay, many a learned, holy, and pious man has come hither from other Mahomedan countries, especially from the two holy cities of Mecca and Medina, who have taken up their abode, and passed their entire lives in this country. Now, if this country were in reality *Darul Harb*, did those venerable men, who were well acquainted with the principles of their religion, mar their good prospects of the other world, and did they continue sinning all the days of their lives? Oh no! They were not such men. Rather, they considered this country as *Darul Islam*, and did not think flight at all incumbent upon them. Similarly, from the commencement of the British rule, all learned Mahomedans of India have considered it unlawful to take interest (on money lent) not only from Mahomedans, but also from infidels. The saying of public prayers on Fridays and on the two Eeds is also observed as duties incumbent upon the faithful. Had this country been *Darul Harb*, the very reverse would have been the case. For it is lawful to take interest from infidels (on money lent) in *Darul Harb*. The saying of public prayers on Fridays and on the two Eeds is prescribed for observance only in *Darul Islam*, but never in *Darul Harb*, in which it is even doubtful whether such public prayers are allowed or not.

Over and above all this, there is one circumstance which deserves the greatest consideration. It is that there is no Mahomedan ruler in the world who is superior to the Sultan of Turkey. He has the honour of being the *khadim* or servant of the two holy cities of Mecca and Medina; and all Mahomedans look upon him as the head of their religion. Great cordiality and friendship exist between him and the British government; and to such an extent, that, when the great war broke out between Russia and Turkey, the British nation rendered valuable assistance to the sultan; they joined him, and fought against the Russians, notwithstanding that the latter were their brother Christians. Now, from this, it is evident that the British government is a true friend of the Mahomedans, and is always inclined to assist them. Although this may not be an argument to prove that British India is *Darul Islam*; it is, however, a sufficient argument to show that jihad against the British nation is unlawful and prohibited; for this nation is an ally of the sultan, and has friendship with him; consequently it cannot be lawful for Mahomedans to make jihad on an ally of the sultan.

Moulvie Fazli Ali ended by saying that, on a perusal of the *fatwah* delivered by the learned men of Lucknow and Delhi on a question put to them by Syud Ameer Hossain of Bhaugulpore, which has been published in several of the Oordoo newspapers, it is clear that an oversight has been committed both by the party that put the question, and by those who answered it. First, because in the question, he says, "where the Mahomedans have not the means of waging war with their rulers; and war, if waged, would merely result in bringing the cause of Islam into disrepute…" Now, if British India be considered *Darul Islam*, the above conditions are quite irrelevant and unnecessary. To anyone that possesses the least acquaintance with the Mahomedan law, this oversight will appear too glaring to escape notice. Secondly, those who have answered the question have supposed the Mahomedans of India to be *mustamins*,[38] (or those who have taken protection under a Christian government); and, for this reason, they have declared jihad to be unlawful in this country. But the fact is that Mahomedans cannot be held to be *mustamin*s, except when they are in *Darul Harb*. So that, if the Mahomedans of British India be deemed *mustamin*s, then it will follow that British India must be *Darul Harb*. But it has been fully established

38. A *must'amin* is a foreigner who has received a safe conduct (*amān*) which gives him permission to live or travel for a limited duration in another land. His position is analogous to that of a modern visa holder.

by the clear authorities of the Mahomedan law that British India is *Darul Islam*; and this decision has not been arrived at among Mahomedans today only, but has been understood ever since the establishment of British rule in this country.

Moulvie Abdool Hakeem rose and said that he proposed a vote of thanks to Moulvie Karamat Ali on behalf of the society for the very able lecture which he had delivered. He then said that he would take advantage of the opportunity to say a few words that appeared to him suitable to the occasion. First, he fully concurred in whatever has been advanced by Moulvie Karamat Ali; and thought there was nothing in the lecture on which men of learning held a different opinion. In all books of Mahomedan law that can be procured in this country, and some of which have been named by the lecturer, the question of *Darul Islam* was treated in exactly the same manner, as in the *Fatawa Alamgeeree*, the composition and language alone being different from one another. Hence, there lived in this country thousands of learned men amongst the Mahomedans who, from the commencement of the British rule, have considered this country as *Darul Islam*, and always conducted themselves as the residents of such, and this country is still considered and treated as such. The cause of this is obvious; for, notwithstanding that their rulers are Christians, they have yet passed no law or regulation which interferes with the Mahomedan religion, and the effect of which would be to change the character of the country from *Darul Islam* into *Darul Harb*.

The previous speakers had not given a detailed account of the circumstances connected with the publication of the *fatwah*; and he (the moulvie) would supply the omission. It appears that Syud Ameer Hossain, personal assistant to the commissioner of Bhaugulpore, finding that inquiries were being made into the causes and extent of the Wahabee disaffection, sent a question as to the lawfulness or otherwise of jihad to Muftee Sadoollah, the ablest of the learned Mahomedans of Lucknow; who, during the Mahomedan reign of Lucknow, held the post of muftee, and at the present moment holds both the posts of muftee and kazee at the native state of Rampore. The muftee drew out a *fatwah*, which under his signature he caused to be circulated among the learned men of Delhi and Lucknow; and they too affixed their signatures to it. It was then sent to Syud Ameer Hossain, who forwarded it to most of the Hindoostanee newspapers for publication. An English translation of the same was also forwarded to several of the English Newspapers; and it appeared likewise in their columns. But, before making any comments on the *fatwah* in question, he (Moulvie Abdool Hakeem) would first read it out.

[Question]

Learned men and expounders of the law of Islam! What is your opinion on the following question of Mahomedan law?

In the case, where a Mahomedan country becomes the possession of a Christian power, and such [a] power in no way interferes with the prescribed rites of Islam, such as prayer, fasting, pilgrimage, *zakat*, Friday prayer, and public worship; but accords the same protection, (or civil and religious liberty), as would be granted by a Mahomedan ruler; and where the Mahomedans have not the means of waging war with their rulers; and war, if waged, would merely result in bringing the cause of Islam into disrepute, as is the case in India at the present time; is a jihad lawful or otherwise? Answer the above, quoting authorities, for doing which, may God reward you.

[Reply]

In the above case, the Mahomedans are *mustamin*s under the Christian power; (viz., they are under the protection of their Christian rulers, and in free enjoyment of civil and religious liberty); and it is not lawful for a *mustamin*, who has accepted the conditions of protection or civil and religious liberty, to carry on a jihad; for one of the conditions for carrying on a jihad is the absence of treaty engagements between the Mahomedans and unbelievers, or the refusal by either party to grant protection or civil or religious liberty to the other; and it is also a necessary condition for the carrying on of a jihad that there should be a probability of victory of the Mahomedans, and of power and glory accruing to the cause of Islam. Should such a condition not exist, a jihad is not lawful. The author of the *Manhajul Ghaffar*[39] (a work on Mahomedan law), in laying down the principle, that it is unlawful for a *mustamin* (who has accepted the conditions of protection or civil and religious liberty) to commit an offence against the property, lives, and honour (of his protectors), thus expresses himself:—

"For he by having accepted the conditions of protection (or civil and religious liberty), has taken upon himself an engagement not to commit an offence against them, (i.e. his protectors), and the commission of such an offence by him is treachery, and treachery is unlawful." Again, in the *Fatawa Alamgeeree*, the following passage occurs:—

"The conditions under which it (i.e. jihad) becomes lawful are two; the first being when the enemy rejects the appeal to join the true religion, and no treaty engagements exist between him and ourselves; whether, if protection or civil and religious liberty be granted by one of the two parties to the other; and the second, when he, (who wages a jihad), to the best of his own judgment, or trusting the judgment of one in whose opinion and council he places confidence, expects an accession of glory and power to the cause of the Mahomedans; but, if he does not anticipate an accession of power and glory to the Mahomedans, by waging war, in such a case, war is unlawful on account of the attendant risk of self-destruction — God knows the best."

39. I.e., *Minaḥ al-ghaffār*, cited above.

The moulvie said that it would now appear how much this *fatwah* was inapplicable to the real state of affairs. For, in point of fact, British India is *Darul Islam*, as has already been demonstrated by the gentlemen who preceded him; and, in *Darul Islam*, Mahomedans are not required to seek the protection of the sovereign for the exercise of civil and religious liberty.

Therefore such an epithet as *mustamin*s is inapplicable to the Moslem inhabitants of such a country. *Mustamin* is a technical term applied to a Mahomedan who goes to a *Darul Harb*, there being no safeguard for the free exercise of the civil and religious liberty of true believers; and seeks, and obtains such a guarantee from the sovereign for a temporary period; because it is not lawful for a Mahomedan to pass the whole of his life in *Darul Harb*, even if he obtain protection from the sovereign forever. *Mustamin* is also applied to an infidel who goes to *Darul Islam*; and under similar circumstances, obtains the protection of the sovereign for a fixed period only, and not for the term of his life; for, if he should remain there for the whole period of his life, he becomes a *zimmee*. Now, if the Mahomedans of British India be held to be *mustamin*s, then British India would necessarily be *Darul Harb*; and it would become unlawful for Mahomedans to live in this country for the term of their lives. Nevertheless, it must be admitted, that, on the premises assumed, the *fatwah* was quite in accordance with Mahomedan law. These are the words of the question: – "If the Christian sovereign accords the same protection as would be granted by a Mahomedan sovereign." It is here assumed, according to the technicalities of the Mahomedan law, that the condition of Mahomedans in India is that of *mustamin*s, and the question is put accordingly; that is to say: – whether or not it is lawful for such a Moslem (who is a *mustamin*) to make *jihad* with his Christian sovereign who has granted him protection. The business of a *muftee* is simply to answer a question as put to him; and not to enquire into the accuracy or otherwise of the question;

hence the answer of the learned moulvies, given without inquiry, as to the country of Islam, in regard to which the question was put. True, the questioner uses the qualifying phrase "as is the case in India at the present time;" but it is quite possible to infer that the question has reference either to India, itself, or to some other country which resembles India in certain circumstances. The latter was the more likely view to be taken; and he, the moulvie, was persuaded, that this was actually done by the learned moulvies in framing their answer to it. If, on the other hand, they had been directly asked, "whether British India, under existing circumstances, was *Darul Islam* or *Darul Harb*," those gentlemen would undoubtedly have answered that it was *Darul Islam*. Had they considered it to be *Darul Harb*, they would not have continued in India, quietly with their families and children; nor have observed the prayers of Fridays and the two Eeds. Besides, the speaker had a recollection of having read somewhere that one of the gentlemen who signed the *fatwah* in question, viz., Moulvie Mahomed Kootuboodeen of Delhi, had given a *fatwah* with reference to the mutiny of 1857, in which he held that the war, which the Hindoos and Mahomedans then jointly waged against the British government, was not a jihad but a rebellion. Now no war waged by the Mahomedans can be pronounced to be a rebellion, unless it be against a ruler of *Darul Islam*. It also occurred to the speaker that he had read in some manuscript that Moulvie Shah Abdool Azeez of Delhi, one of the most learned and revered of the Mahomedans whom India has seen for several centuries, delivered a *fatwah* to the effect that British India was *Darul Islam*.[40]

40. If this is the case, it does not seem to have survived.

Sayyid Ahmad Khan: On the Ambiguous Status of India

The classification of British India as either an abode of war or as an abode of Islam was a difficult one because of its high social and political stakes. This is clearly evident in the writings of Sayyid Ahmad Khan (d. 1316/1898), a prominent reformist thinker who vacillated on the issue. An integral part of Sayyid Ahmad's project was the reconciliation of Islamic and Western thought. His views on whether India was part of the abode of war are inconsistent. At one point he attempts to skirt the whole dichotomy between the abode of war and the abode of Islam by arguing for the existence of a third category, which he calls the "*Dar-ul-aman*, or 'land of security,' in which a Moslem may lawfully reside as a *moostamin*, or seeker of *aman*."[41] In classical Islamic law, an "amān" is a document of safe-conduct which a Muslim ruler or his deputy could give to individual residents of the abode of war who wanted to travel in Islamic territory. It could also, in theory, denote a non-Muslim ruler's safe-conduct for a Muslim visitor to his territory. Sayyid Ahmad extends the meaning of this term by suggesting that it can be applied to a whole region, the so-called *Dar-ul-aman*. For him, it is as if all Indian Muslims are recipients of this safe-conduct which binds them in obedience to the British ruler who in return will guarantee their safety. India is thus not an abode of Islam, but it is still a land in which it is impermissible to wage war against the ruler. Sayyid Ahmad is presumably led to this conclusion because of his contention that British India is "a country in which that protection is afforded to the faithful with which they met at the hands of the Christian ruler of Abyssinia;[42] and that consequently, so long as that protection exists, we must conclude that insurrection would be a crime. To call such a country *Dar-ul-harb*,

41. Syed Ahmad Khan Bahadur, "An Article on Jihad, Published in the Editorial Columns of *The Pioneer* of the 23rd November, 1871," in *Review on Dr. Hunter's Indian Musalmans: Are They Bound in Conscience to Rebel Against the Queen?* (Benares: Medical Hall Press, 1872), xix.

42. On this event, see M. Watt, *Muḥammad at Mecca* (Oxford: Oxford University Press, 1953), 115 ff.

in the strict and only legitimate sense of the word, is absurd."[43] Nonetheless, in other places, Sayyid Ahmad does indeed refer to India as an abode of war, albeit one in which the activity of *jihād* is impermissible. He wrote that he rejected the opinion, espoused by Karamat ʿAli in his speech to the Mahomedan Literary Society of Calcutta (included above), that India should be categorized as the abode of Islam. He writes:

> I cannot congratulate the Mahomedan Literary Society of Calcutta on their assertion that India is *Dar-ul-Islam*, and of their thus evading the necessity for rebellion. India, in spite of the Calcutta Mahomedan Literary Society, is *Dar-ul-Harb*, but not in the sense in which the Englishman interprets it. My readers are aware that in *Dar-ul-Islam*, usury is prohibited. Now, a country may be *Dar-ul-Harb* in two senses, 1st, that of its being a foreign country in which it is lawful for Mahomedans to take interest for their money;[44] 2nd, in the sense of its being lawful for the Faithful to make religious war (*jihad*) upon it. India is *Dar-ul-Harb* in the former sense, but not in the latter. Great Britain is *Dar-ul-Harb* as regards usury, but not as regards *jihad*, because the treaty between it and Turkey is binding on the latter.[45]

Thus, despite his legal categorization of British India as an abode of war, Sayyid Ahmad is concerned to promote peace between the British and the Muslim community. He fervently wishes to avoid a confrontation which would cause a loss of life like that which occurred in the 1857 Uprising.[46] Below is an example of one of his attempts at reconciling the British and the Muslims. The work, which is a response to a hypothetical question posed by the colonial

43. Quoted in Ahmad Khan, *Review on Dr. Hunter's Indian Musalmans*, xxxi.

44. Although the taking of interest (*ribā*) is usually prohibited, many Ḥanafī jurists of the classical period granted an exception for transactions occurring in the abode of war. On this, see Abou El Fadl, "Islamic Law and Muslim Minorities," 174.

45. Ahmad Khan, "A Letter from Syed Ahmed Khan Bahadur, C. S. I., to the editor of the Pioneer, published in the issue of the 14th April, 1871," reprinted in Syed Ahmad Khan Bahadur, *Review on Dr. Hunter's Indian Musalmans: Are They Bound in Conscience to Rebel Against the Queen?* (Benares: Medical Hall Press, 1872), x-xi.

46. He describes how the latter event radically changed him: "For some time I wrestled with my grief and, believe me, it made an old man of me. My hair turned white."Altāf Husain Hālī, *Hayat-i-Javed*, tr. David Mathews (Delhi: Rupa and Co, 1994), 84.

official, William Hunter, treads a careful line between support for British rule and solidarity with the Muslim community of India.

Sayyid Ahmad Khan: Indian Muslim Loyalties in Wartime[47]

(1871)

[Question]

Learned men and expounders of the law of Islam! What is your opinion in the following matter? In case of a Mahomedan ruler attacking India while in the possession of the English, is it the duty of the Mahomedans of that country to renounce the *aman* of the English and render help to the invader?

[Answer]

...As long as Musalmans can preach the unity of God in perfect peace, no Musalman can, according to his religion, wage war against the rulers of that country, of whatever creed they be. Next to the Holy Koran, the most authoritative and favourite works of the Wahabis are *Bokhári* and *Muslim*,[48] and both of them say – "When our Prophet Muhammad marched against any infidel people to wage holy war upon them, he stopped the commencement of hostilities till morning, in order to find out whether the *azan* (call for prayer) was being called in the adjacent country. If so, he never fought with its inhabitants." His motive for this was that, from hearing the *azan*, he (the Prophet) could at once ascertain whether the Moslems of the place could discharge their religious duties and ceremonies openly and without molestation. Now we Mahomedans of India live in this country with

47. Hunter, *The Indian Musulmans*, 145.

48. I.e., the two most highly regarded collections of *ḥadīths* (traditions narrated about the Prophet).

every sort of religious liberty; we discharge the duties of our faith with perfect freedom; we read our *azan*s as loud as we wish; we can preach our faith on the public roads and thoroughfares as freely as Christian missionaries preach theirs; we fearlessly write and publish our answers to the charges laid against Islam by the Christian clergy; and even publish works against the Christian faith; and last, though not least, we make converts of Christians to Islam without fear or prohibition.

My reply to Dr. Hunter's question is therefore that in no case would it be the religious duty of any Mahomedan to renounce the *aman* of the English, and render help to the invader. Should they do so, they would be regarded as sinners against their faith, as they would then break that holy covenant which binds subjects to their rulers, and which it is the duty of the former to keep sacred to the last. I cannot, however, predict what the actual conduct of the Musalmans would be in the event of an invasion of India by a Mahomedan or any other power. He would be a bold man indeed who would answer for more than his intimate friends and relations, perhaps not even for them. The civil wars in England saw fathers fighting against sons, and brothers against brothers; and no one can tell what the conduct of a whole community would be in any great political convulsion. I have no doubt, but that the Musalmans would do what their political status – favorable or the contrary – would prompt them to do. I think Dr. Hunter's crucial question might be put to the Hindu as well as to the Mahomedan community. It would be but fair to both parties.

The 1920 Hijrat to Afghanistan

One of the most significant examples of the practice of the obligation of migration (*hijra*) in the Indian subcontinent was the so-called *Hijrat* of 1920, in which thousands of Muslims moved from

British India to Afghanistan.[49] One British observer provides a vivid description of this event. He writes that "whole families, and in some cases whole villages went on Hijrat. Some were too old and infirm to walk, and these were carried in bullock-carts. Walking by the side of the carts could be seen mothers with babies only a few days old. Nearly every company was headed by a musician. One large company was played out of British India to the tune of the British Grenadiers, played on an old fife!"[50] The writer also describes the immense hardships that these migrants met on the way, forcing some of them to turn back. The migration to Afghanistan was closely associated with the Khilafat movement. This movement arose in India in support of the Ottoman caliph, who had been endangered by Britain and other western powers as a result of the dissolution of the Ottoman Empire following World War I.[51] While the movement does not seem to have had broad support among traditional scholars, its leaders required religious backing, which was provided by a variety of reformist thinkers. One such thinker was Muḥyī al-Dīn Aḥmad, better known by his pen name, Abul Kalam Azad (d. 1958). He came from a traditional family of scholars but had been greatly influenced by reformist thinkers including Jamāl al-Dīn al-Afghānī, Rashīd Riḍā, and Sayyid Ahmad Khan. Azad was extensively involved in resistance to British rule. Later in life, he participated in the Indian independence movement as president of the All India National Congress, a movement founded in 1885 and comprised of Hindus, Muslims and others, which campaigned for independence. Azad served as its president from 1940-1947. Despite his earlier views on migration, he decided to remain in

49. During this period, India and Afghanistan shared a border since what is now modern-day Pakistan was then a part of British India.

50. F. S. Briggs, "The Indian Hijrat of 1920," *The Moslem World* 20 (1930), 165. Cf. Dietrich Reetz, *Hijrat: The Flight of the Faithful: A British File on the Exodus of Muslim Peasants from North India to Afghanistan in 1920* (Berlin: Verlag das arabische Buch, 1995), 67 ff.

51. The National Assembly of the Turkish Republic, led by Kemal Ataturk, would "officially" abolish the position of caliph in 1924.

India after the India/Pakistan partition (1947) and became minister of education.[52]

Abul Kalam Azad: Decree of Migration from India[53]
(July 30, 1920)
Translated by Hafeez Malik

After examining all the reasons contained in the *Shari'a,* as well as contemporary events, the interests of the Muslims, and the pros and cons [of political issues], I definitely feel satisfied that, from the viewpoint of the *Shari'a,* the Muslims of India have no choice but to migrate from India. All Muslims who would like to fulfill Islamic obligations must quit India. Those who cannot migrate immediately should help the migrants as if they were themselves migrating from the country. The *Shari'a* gives us no alternative course, except migration.

Migration from India before the war was desirable; now it is mandatory. Only those Muslims can remain in India who are needed to carry on the struggle [for the caliphate] or have acceptable reasons against migration. Large-scale population transfer, however, causes understandable delay. Those who under such circumstances fail to migrate should devote their energy and resources to following the *Shari'a.* They should

52. It is possible that his opinion might have been influenced by the population "exchange" between Turkey and Greece in the 1920s in which the two countries mutually agreed to deport their "religious minority" populations. As a result, about one and a half million Christians were transferred from Turkey to Greece, and nearly half a million Muslims were transferred from Greece to Turkey. Starvation, disease, and violence claimed the lives of many of these migrants.

53. This translation has been reproduced with permission from Hafeez Malik, *Moslem Nationalism in India and Pakistan* (Washington, D. C.: Public Affairs Press, 1963), 343-44. Douglas downplays the significance of this fatwā, see Ian Henderson Douglas, *Abul Kalam Azad: An Intellectual and Religious Biography* (Delhi: Oxford University Press, 1988), 173-74. For a convincing refutation of Douglas's view, see M. Naeem Qureshi, *Pan-Islam in British Indian Politics: A Study of the Khilafat Movement, 1918-1924* (Leiden: Brill, 1999), 189.

organize themselves according to the *Shariʿa,* and should never give up their determination and enthusiasm for migration. Under the present circumstances, the creation of [such a Muslim] party will be a sterling achievement.

It should be understood that the *Shariʿa* does not allow individual and spasmodic migration. Migration should be undertaken collectively and requisite arrangements should be made by the party [organized for migration]. The party chief should decide the following questions: a) who should migrate immediately; b) who should remain behind to render useful services to the cause; and c) the time and place for migration. An individual is not authorized to determine these questions for himself.

When the order for migration is given, migration becomes mandatory. The Prophet Muhammad has left us an exemplary procedure. Before the preparation for migration is made an oath of *bayʿa* [allegiance] must be taken. Due to several reasons (their explanation can be found in *Risalah-i-Hijrat*) not everyone can migrate from India nor is that required by the *Shariʿa.* It is, therefore, obvious that while migration continues, India will not be denuded of its Muslim population. Those who remain in India will be bound by the *Shariʿa* to sever all ties of good will and mutual collaboration with the invaders of Islam. Those who disregard this Qurʾanic injunction will be considered enemies of Islam.

"Good will and mutual collaboration" is my [Azad's] translation of *"mawalat"* which occurs in the Qurʾan.[54] "*Mawalat*" connotes all acts of cooperation, which the caliphate committee rejects according to the "non-cooperation" plan. The cooperation of Muslims with the British government was prohibited by the *Shariʿa* on the day Turkey declared herself at war with the Allied Powers. That is why I endeavored at the Delhi meetings in February and later on

54. The Qurʾān does not use this exact word, although it uses words of the same root to indicate this principle of cooperation.

April 11, 1920, at the Bombay Caliphate Conference to have the non-cooperation plan passed by the [delegates]. Non-cooperation was not decided upon as a defensive measure in case our demands were rejected [by the British government]; it had become mandatory for Muslims since the advent of hostilities. For this reason alone, I endeavored again at the Meerut Caliphate Conference to explain the "why's" of the Muslim obligation relative to non-cooperation with the Government.

This is not just political expediency; I believe in it with all my heart. Although Islam [the Ottoman caliphate] lost all its European areas as well as Baghdad and Damascus, our faith was not endangered. Now the situation has changed. It is not just a question of the defense of Constantinople, our very "faith" is in the balance. We not only want to defend the land, but also seek the survival of our "faith." If we failed to defend Constantinople and Baghdad, we must not fail to protect our *iman* (faith).

I have decided the course of action [non-cooperation] for myself and will follow it steadfastly. All those who seek righteousness *(talib-i haqq)* and trust me should follow me or obtain further instruction from the following persons:

Mawlavi ʿAbdul Qadir, Vakil of Qasur, district Lahore.
Mawlavi Mhyad-ud-Din Ahmad of Qasur, district Lahore.
Mawlana Muhammad Daud Ghazanvi, Amritsar.
Mawlavi ʿAbdur Razaq (Mlhy Abadi), Editor of *al-Byan*, Lucknow.

Risalah-i-Hijrat is being composed and will be published in the near future. Those who still have further questions regarding the import of the *Shariʿa* [on non-cooperation and migration] should wait for its publication.[55]

55. This work does not seem to have ever been composed.

The End of Calls for Migration from India

After the disastrous human casualties of the *hijrat* to Afghanistan, calls for migration do not seem to have been raised frequently in scholarly discourse. Many Muslims did indeed migrate to Pakistan from India after the partition, but they did not do so in response to an Islamic imperative, but as a result of political pressures. The vast majority of India's Muslims, including their leaders, did not leave India. The question of migration as an Islamic obligation was, however, occasionally raised. Shortly after the 1947 partition of India, one Muslim asked Husayn Ahmad Madani, a noted Indian scholar, whether he was obligated to leave for Pakistan. The questioner writes about Hindu persecution of Muslims and describes how Hindus insult the Prophet. He worries about a younger generation of Muslims in India who have become increasingly distanced from their faith which, he says, they have substituted with the teachings of Gandhi. In his response, Madani first establishes that the Prophet's example of migrating to Medina does not apply to the Muslims of India. He analyzes the Prophet's migration thus:

> Think about the life in Mecca before the *hijra*. The devoted friends of the Prophet.... whom you believe to be true... did not emigrate from there before the *hijra*. And even after the *hijra*, ʿAbbās, his sons and family and others remained (in Mecca). The unbelievers were saying and doing all that was possible (against them). They entertained particular animosity towards the Prophet. Still, did he lose his patience and endurance, or did he persevere in upright living... and spreading Islam? Polytheism and idolatry are the greatest sins in Islam. The Prophet saw them; idolatrous temples were in front of him, polytheistic processions and idols were taken out... The Prophet saw and heard all this, yet did not heave a sigh but lived on, saying "To you your religion and to me mine [Qurʾān 109: 6].[56]

56. Y. Friedmann, "The Attitude of the Jamʿiyyat-i ʿUlamāʾ-i Hind to the Indian National Movement and the Establishment of Pakistan," *Asian and African Studies* 7 (1971), 179.

Madani then makes the following points:

(1) A fatwā demanding that all Muslims leave India is exactly what the Hindus want (i.e., it is not aligned with the Muslims' best interests). (2) Even if it was stipulated by Muslim leaders that all Muslims had to leave India, all of them would not leave. Given this situation, Madani says that one must consider what would become of those who remained and concludes that they would no doubt apostatize. (3) Even if all Indian Muslims left, there would be no country which could accommodate them all. He says that Pakistan, the most convenient option, is too poor to do so. (4) Madani blames Muslims for the partition of India/Pakistan. He says that it is the result of those who said, "We wish to rule and to do whatever we please wherever we are in the majority. Let the Hindus rule and do whatever they please wherever they are in the majority." Given this situation, he says that "it is an act of generosity on the part of the Hindus that they establish secularism in the country" rather than Hindu rule. (5) Finally, Madani says that the Muslim leadership of India have made adequate provisions for the Islamic education of its Muslims.[57]

The issue of Islamic life in India continues to be discussed. The sheer volume of the literature, however, precludes its inclusion in this anthology. One major focus of discussion has been the issue of Muslim communal autonomy in the area of family law. The issue was brought to a head when, in 1985, the Supreme Court of India granted Shah Bano, a Muslim divorcée, alimony to which she was not entitled under Islamic family law. In so doing, it limited the communal legal autonomy of the Muslim community by making Muslims subject to the same rules of divorce as the majority, non-Muslim population. The judgment led to massive protests by Muslims who felt that it was an infringement on their communal autonomy and even Shah Bano distanced herself from the judgment's implications. As a result of this, the judgment was

57. A translation of this fatwā is found in ibid., 177-80.

eventually nullified through legislation. The Shah Bano affair, however, is frequently referenced in India since it touches upon many of the issues relating to Muslim communal rights.[58]

58. On views about non-Muslim rule among Muslims in contemporary India, see Muhammad Qasim Zaman, *The Ulama in Contemporary Islam: Custodians of Change* (Princeton: Princeton University Press, 2002), 160 ff. and Yoginder Sikand, *Muslims in India: Contemporary Social and Political Discourses* (Gurgaon: Hope India Publications, 2006). On the Shah Bano Case, see *Encyclopedia of Women & Islamic Cultures: Family, Law, and Politics*, ed. Suad Joseph and Afsaneh Najmabadi, s.v., "Shah Bano Affair."

– 4 –

The French in North Africa

The fall of the Ottoman regency of Algiers to the French in 1830 made an answer to the question of whether Muslims could live under non-Muslim rule a matter of great urgency. Many of the responses to this question concern the Algerian revolutionary, ʿAbd al-Qādir b. Muḥyī al-Dīn al-Jazāʾirī (d. 1300/1883). In 1832, after the French conquest of Algeria, ʿAbd al-Qādir formed a political entity in the town of Mascara and began to set up an Islamic government with a standing army which resisted the French.[1] One of ʿAbd al-Qādir's main concerns was to rally the Muslims of Algeria. He wanted them to migrate from French-controlled areas to his camps and to fight on his behalf. He framed his demands in Islamic terms stating that the Qurʾān, the *ḥadīth* and the jurists all demanded migration (*hijra*) from the abode of war. He is also known to have sent several requests for fatwās to leading Muslim scholars in the hope of soliciting endorsements for his position and securing permission to take action against Muslims who sided with the French. He is concerned both with Muslims who peacefully live under French rule and thus consolidate French power, as well as with Muslims who actively collaborate. In one of his petitions for a fatwā, he asks, hoping for an answer in the affirmative, whether

1. On ʿAbd al-Qādir and his movement, see R. Danziger, *Abd al-Qadir and the Algerians: Resistance to the French and Internal Consolidation* (New York: Homes & Meier Publishers, 1977); A. Bennison, *Jihad and its Interpretations in Pre-Colonial Morocco* (London: Routledge, 2002) and P. Shinar, "ʿAbd al-Qādir and ʿAbd al-Krīm: Religious Influences on their Thought and Action," *Asian and African Studies* 1 (1965), 143 ff.

Muslims who live under French rule, giving the French material support and fighting on their behalf, can be branded apostates. He emotionally describes Muslim soldiers who wear the French *Médaille d'Honneur* which, he says, was their reward for killing Muslims. If such Muslims are indeed apostates, he asks, can they be immediately killed or must they first be given an opportunity to repent? He further asks whether their goods may be confiscated and whether their wives and children may be killed or enslaved.[2] ʿAbd al-Qādir received a mixed response from the *ʿulamāʾ*. Those who lived in Morocco were reluctant to support him because the Moroccan ruler wanted to distance himself from such revolutionaries in order to avoid potential retaliation from the French. Some *ʿulamāʾ* also believed that punishing Algerian Muslims for living under French rule was unjust given what they had already suffered. Below is a response to those who chastise Muslims who live under French rule and demand their migration by Muḥammad Ibn al-Shāhid (d. 1253/1837 or 1255/1839),[3] the *muftī* of Algiers. While the response does not mention its opponents by name, it seems clear from the context that it is to ʿAbd al-Qādir and his followers that it refers. While Ibn al-Shāhid agrees with ʿAbd al-Qādir that it is not desirable for Muslims to live under non-Muslim rule, he chastises him for the damage to the Algerian Muslims that his views would cause if implemented. His treatise thus represents a defense of those who have not migrated from French-controlled lands.

2. Al-Mahdī al-Wazzānī, *al-Nawāzil al-jadīda al-kubrā fī mā li-ahl Fās wa-ghayrihim min al-badw waʾl-qurā al-musammā biʾl-Miʿyār al-jadīd al-jāmiʿ al-muʿrib ʿan fatāwā al-mutaʾakhkhirīn min ʿulamāʾ al-Maghrib* (Rabat: Wizārat al-Awqāf waʾl-Shuʾūn al-Islāmiyya liʾl-Mamlaka al-Maghribiyya, 1996), 10: 291-92.

3. Abū al-Qāsim Saʿd Allāh, *Tārīkh al-Jazāʾir al-thaqāfī min al-qarn al-ʿāshir ilā al-rābiʿ ʿashar al-hijrī* (16-20 m.) (Algiers: al-Sharika al-Waṭaniyya, 1981), 2: 284-85.

Ibn al-Shāhid: On the Muslims of French Algeria (1830s)[4]

It is... your duty to ask us about our circumstances. Have we been afflicted with religious corruption? Has prayer and the call to prayer ceased from our remaining mosques? Has recitation of the Qur'ān been suspended? Are children prohibited from reading in their schools? Is animal slaughter, marriage and inheritance as it previously was, such that the accursed unbeliever does not interfere at all in it? If this is objectively demonstrated, what we say has been confirmed, that is, that we are able to uphold religion. It is then your duty to ask why we remain in this land. Is it out of contentment with unbelief or love of associating with its people or is it for another reason? How can you imagine that we approve of unbelief and love associating with unbelievers when prices have risen, our industries have been disrupted, our shops have been destroyed, turning a profit has become difficult, our graves have been dug up and the tombs of our saints have been desecrated? These things came to pass only because of their invasion. So what glory is there in this such that we would approve of it?

You have directed your dispute to the scholars and students, so let us begin with them. We say: It is known to everyone that the students have no occupation but earn their living from endowments (*aḥbās*), like those of the mosques, by [conducting] litanies, the call to prayer and prayer leadership. Some of them might perhaps have a shop where they buy and sell but which does not impede their learning, and perhaps some of them have another house or orchard left to them by their grandparents, and perhaps some have inherited from someone who died, but their mainstay is the endowments. Therefore, the rich among them is someone who has, more

4. Published in Muḥammad ʿAbd al-Karīm, *Ḥukm al-hijra min khilāl thalāth rasāʾil jazāʾiriyya* (Algiers: al-Sharika al-Waṭaniyya liʾl-Nashr waʾl-Tawzīʿ, 1981), 105-124.

or less, twenty or thirty dinars in his storehouse. Under these circumstances, how can it be easy for him to travel?!

"Travel is a portion of punishment," as [the Prophet], may God bless him and grant him peace, said, even though [the *ḥadīth*] is an isolated one. You say that migration is easily accomplished. Then, if a person wants to travel, he must do so either by land or by sea. Let us select the first option and discuss it. How can travel be easy for anyone when he is traveling with his wife, children, servants and belongings? Assuming that he is poor, as we have mentioned, he will need beasts to carry his belongings. Perhaps he will have sufficient means to rent these beasts, but despite that, he will not be safe from being robbed of his belongings and killed together with those who are with him, as has happened many times. Are any of you able to provide a guarantee to a migrant that he will not be robbed and killed? Then, if we assume that he reaches a town or some such place, with what will he make a living, since he presumably has no occupation? Do you order that he return to his land or that he remain a beggar in yours? This is the same whether he travels to the villages or whether he travels to the mountains in which there is what we have mentioned and, in addition, there is the gathering of provisions of wood, water and flour since these things are not easy in the mountains… As for travel by sea, what we have mentioned regarding travel by land is true except that renting a mode of travel for the sea is more expensive and is safer than travel by land.

This is what pertains to the students. As for the common people, some of them, like the students, are poor and some of them are not. Some wealthy people remain, but most have traveled from this land, by land or by sea, to the east and to the west, as everyone can see. Those who remain have different reasons for delaying their travels. Some of them have real estate that they want to sell, but this has not been easy for them, and some of them have debts and do not want to travel until they have collected them, and some of them have

> many families who depend on them and await the time when it will be easy for them to travel away. The migration of the companions of the Prophet, may God bless him and grant him peace, was not accomplished in a day or in a single month; rather, they migrated at a time when it was easy for them to do so, and we are in the same position. All the people without exception have the intent to travel and leave, all wait in anticipation of the time in which it will be easy for them. This then is the reason for our remaining in this land. As for what you have heard about some people who have become helpers and servants of the unbeliever, they have been prompted to do this out of love of the world, and God knows what is in their hearts: "You do not guide whom you love, but God guides whom He wills" (Qur'ān 28: 56).
>
> [The above] is what pertains to the matter of migration. You were not, [however], content in your treatise with pronouncing us unbelievers until you had slandered our women and children [by alleging that they] consort with the unbelievers ... If by "fornication" you mean the fornication of the prostitutes... we say that fornication was already widespread both among us and among other [Muslim societies] before this at a time when Islam[ic government] was present, and you did not change that or censure it then. If you were to say we did not have control over it then, we would respond, we do not have the power to change it now.[5]

Muḥammad b. Aḥmad ʿIllaysh on the Muslims of French Algeria

Muḥammad b. Aḥmad ʿIllaysh of Egypt (d. 1299/1882) was an outspoken opponent of European influence in Egypt.[6] Later in life, this led him to participate in the ʿUrābī Revolt (1881-82) against

5. Ibid., 118-119.

6. For his biography, see Gilbert Delanoue, *Moralistes et politiques musulmans dans l'Égypte de XIXème siècle* (Cairo: Institut Français d'Archéologie Orientale, 1982), 127-140.

the British which resulted in his apprehension by the authorities and death in prison. ʿIllaysh's strong support for ʿAbd al-Qādir's position was perhaps made easier by his location in Egypt, far removed from the Algerian crisis. Unlike the jurists of Fez who had to take into account the opinion of the Moroccan sultan, whose territory ʿAbd al-Qādir abutted and who wanted to avoid confrontation with the French, ʿIllaysh was free to form his own opinion on the matter which was, at the time, of little concern in Egypt. ʿIllaysh's response is squarely in the realm of legal theory, uncomplicated by concerns of practice and implementation. In response to the question regarding migration from French-controlled territory, he simply quotes al-Wansharīsī's (d. 914/1508) fatwās relating to the Spanish Reconquista (translated above) on the assumption that the realities experienced by al-Wansharīsī were no different from those experienced by the Muslims of Algeria, several hundred years later. The question posed to ʿIllaysh is asked anonymously, but it is likely that it was written by ʿAbd al-Qādir or one of his followers.[7]

ʿIllaysh: On the Muslims of French Algeria[8]
(c. 1840)

[Question]

What is your opinion regarding a Muslim region that, having been attacked, conquered and ruled by the unbelieving enemy, still has some mountains on its border that have not been reached and overpowered and are still protected by its peoples. Some of the residents of this area have migrated to it with their families, property and progeny while others have remained under the rule of the unbelievers. The unbelievers

7. On ʿAbd al-Qādir's probable authorship, see Rudolph Peters, *Islam and Colonialism: The Doctrine of Jihad in Modern History* (The Hague: Mouton Publishers, 1979), 58 and 182 n.58.

8. Muḥammad ʿIllaysh, *Fatḥ al-ʿalī al-mālik fī al-fatāwā ʿalā madhhab al-Imām Mālik* (Beirut: Dār al-Maʿrifa, 1978), 375-387.

have imposed a tax upon their subjects which resembles the well-known poll tax (*jizya*).

There are scholars (*ʿulamāʾ*) both among those who migrated and among those who remained. There is a dispute between these two groups of scholars. Those who migrated with the Muslims to the aforementioned mountains say that migration is obligatory. They rule that it is permissible to shed the blood, expropriate the property and take captive the families and progeny of those Muslims who remain under the unbelievers while having the ability to migrate. They base themselves on the fact that someone who remains [necessarily] comes to help in fighting and plundering the Muslims and in striving for the victory of the unbelievers. Those scholars who remain under [the rule of] the unbelievers and do not migrate say that migration is not obligatory. In general, they draw proof for this from His statement, may He be exalted, "If you do this to protect yourselves against them" (Qurʾān 3: 28),[9] and upon the statement of [the Prophet], may God bless him and grant him peace, "There is no migration after the conquest,"[10] and other such traditions.[11] Benefit us with a complete answer with unequivocal proof and which is incontestable and there will be a reward for you from the King, the Bestower.

He answered with this:

[ʿIllaysh's answer is to quote al-Wansharisi's two fatwās on the Muslims of Christian Spain, one of which has been translated above.]

9. The full verse reads: "Let not the believers take unbelievers as allies to the exclusion of believers. Whoever does so has no connection with God. However, this is not the case if you do this to protect yourselves against them. God warns you to beware of Him. To God is the journeying." Thus, according to the reasoning of these scholars, Muslims are given a special dispensation to ally themselves with the French because they do this only to protect themselves against them.

10. For example, *Ṣaḥīḥ al-Bukhārī*, no. 2783 and *Ṣaḥīḥ Muslim* (Beirut: Dār al-Kutub al-ʿIlmiyya, 2003), no. 1353.

11. Muḥammad b. Aḥmad ʿIllaysh, *Fatḥ al-ʿalī al-mālik fī al-fatāwā ʿalā madhhab al-Imām Mālik* (Beirut: Dār al-Maʿrifa, n.d.), 375 ff.

Fatwās for the French

Many of the fatwās supporting French rule in North Africa were initiated not by the conquered Muslims of Algeria, but by French officials. Unlike other Western colonial powers with Muslim subjects, France wished, from a very early stage, to present itself as Muslim. This approach to colonialism was perhaps first exhibited when Napolean conquered Egypt in 1798. Shortly after he landed, he made a declaration to the Egyptians which opened with the traditional Islamic blessings and stated, "I worship God more than the Mamlūks do; and I respect His prophet Muḥammad and the admirable Qurʾān…, the qāḍīs, shaykhs, imāms… tell the people that the French are also true Muslims."[12] By the twentieth century, the French were frequently speaking of France as a "puissance musulmane," or "Muslim power." Even as late as the mid-twentieth century, some French subjects continued to do so. Thus one Muslim scholar hailed France as the "only great Islamic power in the West."[13] A key part of achieving recognition as a Muslim power meant that France attempted to build strong relationships with Muslim scholars and actively solicited fatwās from them in support of its colonial activities.

The main French experience of governing Muslims was in Algeria. It began in 1830 with the surrender of the Ottoman Dey and ended in 1962. One of the earliest officials to solicit a fatwā in favor of French rule was the diplomat Léon Roches, who secured one from jurists belonging to the Tijāniyya *ṣūfī* order, and later had it ratified by jurists from Mecca and the famous al-Azhar seminary in Egypt. The fatwā affirmed that, since everything possible had already been done by the Muslims of Algeria to oppose the French, it was now permissible to temporarily allow them to rule and it was wrong to revolt against them. Only Roches' excerpted French translation of the fatwā remains extant. It reads:

---

12. J. Christopher Herold, *Bonaparte in Egypt* (New York: Harper and Row, 1963), 69 ff.

13. Quoted in David Robinson, *Paths of Accommodation: Muslim Societies and French Colonial Authorities in Senegal and Mauritania, 1880-1920* (Athens: Ohio University Press, 2000), 267.

> When a Muslim people, whose territory has been invaded by the unbelievers, has fought them as long as it retained hope of driving them out, and when it is certain that the continuation of war can only bring misery, ruin and death for Muslims with no chance of defeating the unbelievers, the people, while maintaining the hope of shaking off their yoke with the help of God, accept to live under their rule, on the express condition that they retain the free exercise of their religion and that their wives and daughters will be respected.[14]

Thus, according to the fatwā, non-Muslim rule was to be tolerated providing that it allowed Islam to be freely observed, respected the honor of Muslim women and providing also that there was no prospect of defeating the unbelievers.[15]

After Roches, the gathering of fatwās in support of the French became more widespread.[16] Below are some that appear in a work which came to serve as a textbook for French colonial officials.

Fatwās Compiled by French Colonial Officials in Algiers)[17]
(c. 13th/19th century)

Fatwā 1:
[Question]

The questions posed are three in number and concern Muslims established in a region which the unbelievers have conquered, but which is administered without creating the least

14. Léon Roches, *Dix ans à travers l'Islam: 1834-1844* (Paris: Perrin et cie, 1904), 241.

15. Some have questioned the authenticity of this fatwā on the grounds that there are no references to it other than in Roches' travelogue. While this may be the case, later French officials managed to obtain very similar fatwās. See Marcel Émerit, "La légende de Léon Roches," *Revue Africaine* 91 (1947), 81 ff. and Jean-Pierre Lehmann, "Léon Roches – Diplomat Extraordinary in the Bakumatsu Era: An Assessment of His Personality and Policy," *Modern Asian Studies* 14 (1980), 279 n.18.

16. David Robinson, *Paths of Accommodation*, 268.

17. The fatwās below are found in Octave Depont and Xavier Coppolani, *Les Confréries religieuses musulmanes* (Algiers: Jourdan, 1897), 34 ff. They are translated from the French.

obstacle to the exercise of the Islamic religion and that even encourages Muslims to practice their religious obligations. [The conqueror] gives them, to fulfill the functions of a judge, one of their own Muslim coreligionists, who is charged with executing the prescriptions of Islamic law. He provides this functionary with suitable remuneration which he regularly receives at the start of each month.

Under such circumstances, must the Muslims

1. Emigrate?
2. Go to war against unbelievers and seek to remove their authority, even if they are not certain that they have the power to do so?
3. Must the region which the unbelievers have conquered be considered as a land of Islam or as a land in a state of war?

[Answer]

Here is the response of the chief jurisconsult of Mecca:

Our wise master,[18] may God be merciful to him, has already made known to us his opinion in responding to the following question which had been asked of him: "Is a Muslim required to emigrate from a region in which, for some reason, he is not able to fulfill all of the obligations which his religion imposes?"

His response is conceived in these terms:

One who is not able to discharge the prescriptions which his religion renders obligatory must migrate from the region in which he is located, if he is in a condition to do so, that is to say, if he has the means sufficient to allow him to change his residence. In speaking of people who have converted to Islam and who have not, although having the means to do so, emigrated, God has said: "As for those whom the angels take in death while they wrong themselves, [the angels] will ask: 'In what circumstances were you?' They will say: 'We were oppressed in the land.' [The angels] will say: 'Was not God's

18. It is not clear to which Islamic authority this refers.

earth spacious that you could have migrated therein?'" (Qur'ān 4: 97). Thus God did not excuse these people while they remained there. If, however, they are weak and incapable of migrating to another region, He grants them an exemption in the following verse: "Except for the oppressed among the men, women, and children who are unable to devise a plan and are not guided to a way" (Qur'ān 4: 98). This amounts to saying that hellfire will be home to all of those who refuse to migrate, at least for those who do not number among the oppressed men, women and children, because these are incapable of finding a device which would permit them to flee, that is to say, that due to their physical frailty or their extreme poverty, they are not in a condition to start upon their way or, in other words, to recognize the path that they should follow. It is these that God pardons if they do not migrate. Here ends the answer of our wise master.

The most eminent Qur'ānic commentators have expressed the same opinion and the Prophet, may God bless him and grant him peace, said: "Whosoever, for the sake of his religion, leaves a land to go to another, even if in so doing he has not traversed the distance of a hand span, has merited Paradise and will be the companion of his forefather Abraham and his descendants including Muḥammad, may God grant him all of his blessings."

In the *Miʿrāj al-Dirāya*,[19] according to Mebrout [sic], one finds the following: "Lands in the unbelievers' hands remain Islamic and do not become territories in a state of war when the latter have not made their laws prevail and where, on the contrary, they appoint Muslim judges and officials to whom they [the Muslims] are subject, whether or not this is voluntary." In effect, in every city where there is a Muslim leader, it is permissible for him to administer the Friday prayer, to celebrate religious holidays and to apply Islamic legal penal-

19. I.e., the *Miʿrāj al-dirāya fī sharḥ al-Hidāya* by Muḥammad b. Muḥammad al-Kākī (d. 749/1348).

ties. If the officials are unbelievers, it is still permissible for Muslims to observe the Friday prayer and to choose from among themselves a judge mutually agreed upon by all believers. However, they must then ask that they be given a Muslim leader.

In the *Tanwīr al-Abṣār*[20] and in its commentary, *al-Durr al-mukhtār*,[21] it is said: "One of the following three conditions is necessary for a territory of Islam to become a territory in a state of war. It must (1) either be that the laws of the unbelievers are in force; (2) that the land is annexed to a land which is in a state of war; or (3) that there must not remain a single Muslim or a *dhimmī* who enjoys the first [kind of] security, that which guarantees his existence.

The celebrated al-Ṭahṭāwī[22] glossed this passage from which it clearly follows that wherever the law of the Muslims is applied at the same time as that of the unbelievers, that land is not considered a territory in a state of war.

From everything that we have said, one sees that the moment there is a Muslim judge, [even if] he is appointed by the unbelievers, and Islamic law is applied, as has been said above, a land does not cease to be a land of Islam. And God knows best.

These lines have been written by order
of the servant of the Islamic law,
the jurisconsult of the glorious city of Mecca.

Fatwā 2:
[Answer]

Here is the response of a Shāfiʿī *muftī*, which is much more explicit than the first:

Praise to the One God, may God grant his blessings to our Master Muḥammad, to his family, to his companions and to

20. A work by Muḥammad b. ʿAbdallāh Khaṭīb al-Tamartāshī (1004/1595).
21. A work by Muḥammad b. ʿAlī al-Ḥaṣkafī (d. 1088/1677).
22. I.e., the Egyptian scholar, Aḥmad b. Muḥammad al-Ṭahṭāwī (d. 1231/1816).

all of those after him who go upon the right path. Oh my God, be our guide in the search for the truth.

In the fatwā of the wise Shaykh Muḥammad b. Sulaymān al-Kurdī [d. 1194/1780], the author of a remarkable gloss on Ibn Ḥajar [al-Haytāmī (d. 974/1566)]'s commentary, one finds:[23]

The residence of Muslims in a territory belonging to unbelievers can fall into one of the following four categories: (1) It is obligatory where Muslims can avoid and segregate themselves[24] from unbelief, but in which they have no hope of a Muslim victory. This is because this land is an "abode of Islam," but if they migrate, it will become an abode of war. (2) It is recommended where they are able to openly manifest their religion (*dīn*) and in which they hope that Islam will become openly manifested there.[25] (3) It is reprehensible where they are able [to exercise their religion], but cannot anticipate [a Muslim victory]. (4) It is forbidden where the Muslims cannot openly manifest their religion. Consequently, if the open manifestation of religion and Islamic laws, such as the penalties (*ḥudūd*), etc., are the cause of the destruction of the land or the killing of Muslims—because the unbelievers' officials alone exercise authority without taking into account the injunctions of Islamic law—it is forbidden for Muslims to remain in such a land and migration is obligatory except for someone who is incapable of doing so and is thus excused.

...This responds to the first part of the question which was posed. As for the second part, one must respond that it is not obligatory to go to war with the unbelievers when one is not

23. What follows is corrupt in the French translation and has been corrected on the basis of the original fatwā by al-Kurdī contained in ʿAbd al-Raḥmān Bā ʿAlawī, *Bughyat al-mustarshidīn fī talkhīṣ fatāwā baʿḍ al-aʾimma min al-ʿulamāʾ al-mutaʾakhkhirīn maʿa ḍamm fawāʾid jamma min kutub shattā liʾl-ʿulamāʾ al-mujtahidīn* (Beirut: Dār al-Maʿrifa liʾl-Ṭibāʿa waʾl-Nashr, 1978), 254-55.

24. Presumably what is envisioned is a situation in which Muslims have full communal autonomy.

25. The French translation reads: "and in which they hope that this land will one day be returned to their coreligionists."

capable of achieving success. Finally, for the third part, the response to make is that Islamic land does not become territory in a state of war solely on the basis of its conquest by unbelievers. And God knows best.

Written by one who places all his hope in God,
Muḥammad Saʿīd Ibn Muḥammad,
Shāfiʿī muftī of Mecca.[26]

Fatwās for the French in Mauritania

The most detailed fatwā permitting French rule over Muslims and discouraging their rebellion was by Shaykh Sidia Baba of Mauritania (d. 1346/1927). Shaykh Sidia came from a prominent family of scholars and built a close relationship with the French officials which the latter greatly valued. In a 1904 report, the colonial official, Xavier Coppolani, said of him:

> Cheikh Sidia, whose devotion to the French cause cannot be overestimated, and who is considered by everyone to be the imam of the country, launched a veritable campaign in favor of the pacification of Saharan Mauritania by the French, the only power able to achieve this goal, and developed his arguments from religious precepts and Muslim law against the propaganda in favor of *jihād*.[27]

One French official was even moved to write: "He is a completely different type of human being than the marabouts that I have seen up until now… Even in Europe, he would appear sophisticated, well-spoken, cool, and calm. He is a schoolmaster, a moral authority, an Arab scholar of the olden days, a 'marabout for the

26. Muḥammad Saʿīd b. Muḥammad Bā Baṣīl (d. 1330/1911), see ʿAbdallāh b. ʿAbd al-Raḥmān al-Muʿallimī, *Aʿlām al-Makkīyyin min al-qarn al-tāsiʿ ilā al-qarn al-rābiʿ ʿashar al-hijrī* (Mecca: Muʾassasat al-Furqān li'l-Turāth al-Islāmī, 2000), 1: 250.
27. Robinson, *Paths of Accommodation*, 274-75.

Whites.'"[28] The shaykh worked closely with the French to achieve the "pacification" of Mauritania and his high social status gave his position on cooperation with the French considerable support among Muslims.[29] Nonetheless, there were Muslim scholars who opposed him. One, for example, wrote to him in 1906, "They tell us many things about you. They even say that you remain friends with the unbelievers, despite the fact that you could save yourself from them, just as the Prophet left his country and people to avoid staying among the unbelievers."[30] It is impossible to know with certainty what led Shaykh Sidia to accommodate and build friendships with French colonial officials. His logic for accommodating the French in the fatwā below, however, is quite clear: In the face of the overwhelming power of the French, abandoning armed resistance is essential to avoiding a human catastrophe.

Shaykh Sidia: On Cooperating with the French[31]
(January 5, 1903)

[Question]

Is it necessary for Muslims to wage holy war when Christians occupy their territory and when not only do they [the

28. Geneviève Désiré-Vuillemin, *Contribution à l'histoire de la Mauritanie de 1900 à 1934* (Dakar: Éditions Clairafrique, 1962), 197. Quoted in Robinson, *Paths of Accommodation*, 185.

29. Robinson, *Paths of Accommodation*, 179.

30. Ibid., 311.

31. The fatwā below is translated into English from a French translation as the Arabic original was not accessible. The French translation was published in E. Michaux-Bellaire, "Une Fetoua de Cheikh Sidia: Approuvé par Cheikh Saad Bouh ben Mohammed El Fâdil ben Mamin, frère de Cheikh Mâ El ʿAïnin," *Archives Marocaines* 11 (1907), 132-139. Shaykh Sidia wrote many fatwās prohibiting rebellion against the French. A manuscript copy of one of these ("Fatwa di Sidiyya baba al-qadi di Shinquit (Chinguetti) nel 1903," Institut mauritanien de recherché scientifique, IMRS, 1903, note 447) is referred to in Adriana Piga, *Les voies du soufisme au sud du Sahara* (Paris: Karthala, 2006), 176. It is not clear whether or not this fatwā is the same as the one which appears in the *Archives Marocaines*.

French] not oppose anything affecting religion but, on the contrary, favor the practice of this religion by establishing judges and judicial administration. One should also consider that the Christians act thus towards Muslims for whom the making of holy war is a physical impossibility, just as it is for those [Muslims] who live east of the Maghrib (in Algeria and Tunisia).

Praise God, Master of the Worlds. Blessings and peace upon our lord, Muḥammad the Prophet, upon all our lords, the prophets, and upon all the saints.

[Answer]

It is obligatory for Muslims who find themselves in such conditions not to attack the Christians and to neglect nothing for the sake of living in peace with them. As the Law and the commentaries stipulate, they must not needlessly exhaust themselves in making war against the Christians. The Shaykh Khalīl [d. 767/1365] said in his *Mukhtaṣar*:

It is the prerogative of the ruler to make a truce for the benefit of the Muslims, unless in order to obtain it he becomes subject to certain conditions, for example, being required to abandon a Muslim (prisoner with the Christians).[32] The duration of the peace is not limited, but it is preferred that it not be concluded for more than four months. In a case where Christian treachery is evident, the ruler must keep watch on them. All the conditions of the treaty must be executed, even if this obligates him to give back hostages, whether these are hostages who will convert to Islam or whether they have already converted and have been sent [by the Christians] as hostages, but have not been imprisoned or guarded [by the Muslims].

32. Although the word "Christians" appears in this translation, it does not appear in Khalīl's original work. See *Mukhtaṣar Khalīl*, ed. Ṭāhir Aḥmad al-Zāwī (Cairo: Dār Iḥyā᾽ al-Kutub al-ʿArabiyya, n.d.), 119. It is therefore either the interpolation of Shaykh Sidia or of the French translator.

Benefits should be equal for both parties, otherwise the treaty should not be negotiated, as ʿAbd al-Bāqī [al-Zurqānī (d. 1099/ 1688)] and [Muḥammad b. ʿAbdallāh] al-Kharshī [d. 1104/1690] have said.

He (Khalīl) said: It is permissible [to make a treaty] even in exchange for money – this is a concession for facilitating its application. It is nonetheless established that if the treaty is not free from conditions which contradict the Law, it is void. If the payment of money is a cause of harm to the Muslims, it must be rejected, unless they are unable to do otherwise, and under such circumstances this act is valid.[33]

The ruler (*imām*) cannot give money lest it appear that the Christians have replaced the Muslims. This, in effect, inverts the blessings of the Divine Law which has given Muslims the privilege of levying the *jizya* (poll-tax on non-Muslims). This privilege exists even in the case where it is inexpedient for Muslims to take advantage of it.

When the tribes surrounded Medina, the Prophet, may God bless him and grant him peace, consulted Saʿd b. Muʿādh and Saʿd b. ʿUbayda regarding whether the *Anṣār* [Helpers][34] could relinquish booty to the idolaters (in order to obtain peace) if it was feared that they had become weary in battle. They responded: "If this idea is from God, may He be exalted, we will obey His word. However, the idolaters, in their ignorance of civilization, should not profit from any part of the booty gained by the believers, unless it is by purchase or out of a desire to be hospitable. Without this, what benefit do we have from Islam which God has given us?" The Messenger of God, may God glorify and bless him, saw that they were resolute in battle and renounced his plan. If giving something in order to avoid harm was against the Divine Law, the Prophet would not have asked the opinion of the Anṣār.

33. The French edition follows this statement with "(Arafal El Mazari)." Perhaps this is to indicate that Ibn ʿArafa and al-Māzarī were of this opinion.

34. The *Anṣār* (the Helpers) were those native Medinans who helped Muḥammad and his Meccan companions once they had migrated to Medina.

[Muḥammad b. Aḥmad] Ibn Ghāzī [al-Miknāsī al-Fāsī (d. 919/1513)] reproduced verbatim the words of [Muḥammad b. ʿAlī] al-Māzarī [d. 536/1141] on this subject which must be reported here. This constitutes the best argument in favor of the words of the *Muṣannaf.*

Bensani [sic][35] said: "Peace is without limits," that is to say that there are no obligatory limits. This does not contradict the principle, "it is preferred that it should not be concluded for more than four months." The prolonging of the peace is permitted if one surmises that this prolonging would serve to augment the power of the Muslims and their territory.

It is necessary that the benefits be reciprocal during this period of peace. However, he must do what is most advantageous. Such is the opinion of ʿAbd al-Bāqī, al-Kharshī and al-Sūdānī.[36] Sīdī Khalīl added: "Except in the case of war, that is to say, when a danger is feared. It is licit in this case, on the part of the ruler, to pay money to the unbelievers. The Muslims, in effect, find themselves in the position of prisoners in their hands, and remitting money becomes licit just like redeeming a prisoner by way of paying a ransom."

Shaykh Khalīl, in his *Mukhtaṣar*, also said: "At the time of conquest, one can authorize the construction of a church if this is stipulated in the treaty, but not otherwise. One can also restore ruined (churches) to someone who has obtained such [treaty] stipulations. One can authorize the construction of a church and one can sell land for the construction of a church with a wall, except in an Islamic town, unless this is necessary to avoid a greater harm."[37] That is to say, the con-

35. It is possible that the author refers to Aḥmad b. Yaḥyā Ibn Sanī al-Dawla (d. 658/1260).

36. It is possible that the author refers to Aḥmad b. ʿUmar al-Sūdānī (d. 971/1563).

37. The French version, translated above, is not identical to the Arabic printed version. See *Mukhtaṣar Khalīl*, 118. For an analysis of Khalīl's statement in the light of the views of other jurists, see M. Perlmann, *Shaykh Damanhūrī on the Churches of Cairo (1739)* (Berkeley: University of California Press, 1975), 33 ff.

struction of a church is permissible in a case where it constitutes the lesser of two harms, as one finds in ʿAbd al-Bāqī, al-Kharshī and al-Sūdānī.

Sīdī Khalīl said: "Except in an Islamic town" – even if (the Christians) were to pay the land's weight in gold – except in order to avoid a greater harm than the establishment of this church. In that case, one can let it be established, thus choosing the lesser of two harms. It is a general obligation, an absolute rule, conforming to the traditions, prescribed on many occasions by Khalīl's commentators, and in other works of jurisprudence. All the authors are unanimous on this point in order to achieve the greatest possible benefit and, between two harms, to choose the lesser one. It is evident according to this that the obligation of holy war disappears where it is incapable of being made.

God said: "The weak, the sick and those who find nothing to spend are not at fault if they are true to God and His messenger. There is no ground [for complaint] against those who do good. God is forgiving and merciful" (Qurʾān 9: 91).

According to Khalīl's *Mukhtaṣar*, the obligations [of *jihād*] do not exist except for one who is free, male and adult, etc. All the authors agree in this respect.

The impotence of this country to do battle against the Christian power is recognized. All people of sense, who listen and who see, realize the lack of unity of the Muslims, the absence of a state treasury, which is indispensable for all actions, and the inferiority of their armies compared to those of the Christians. Thus they are not only excused from conducting holy war but are also commanded not to do so. Also, the obligation of migration is not imposed, either collectively or individually, from territory conquered by the unbelievers, both because of their poverty and because of the lack of places to which they could migrate and where they would find security and the necessary resources.

God said: "Except for the oppressed among the men, women, and children, who are unable to devise a plan and are not shown a way" (Qur'ān 4: 98-99). God will pardon them,[38] He is pardoning and forgiving.

[Najm al-Dīn] al-Nasafī [d. 537/1142] said: "Unable to devise a plan," that is to say, given their poverty and powerlessness. And, "are not shown a way," that is to say, they have no knowledge of the roads.

ʿAbdallāh b. ʿUmar al-Bayḍāwī [d. c. 710/1310] said: "Unable to devise a plan," that is to say, finding the means necessary to make it succeed. As for, "are not shown a way," it concerns knowledge of the roads, either by way of landmarks or through guides, as other commentators have also said.

If the idea of migration comes from God, it is obligatory because the Merciful One, if He gives rise to the idea of a thing, that thing becomes an obligation. This is what was said by al-Nasafī and by other commentators.

It should be further noted that the conduct of Christians, as stated in the question, is such that they not only do not object to the exercise of [the Islamic] religion, but [also] lend it their assistance by building mosques, appointing qāḍīs, and making everything well-organized. They suppress robbery and brigandry, keep peace among the rebellious tribes of this ungoverned country, and do many other things of this nature – and it is obvious that they are very successful in this.

God, may He be exalted, in His mercy and goodness, has sent them for all creation. All creation belongs to Him and all rely upon Him. God said: "God does not forbid you to deal kindly and justly with those who have not fought against you on account of religion and have not driven you out from your homes" (Qur'ān 60: 8). God loves righteous men. You should honor them, be generous with them, and respect them in both word and action. This is what al-Nasafī said. God said: "Unless you have no trust in them."[39] In [the commen-

38. The Qur'ānic passage says that God *may* pardon them.
39. It is unclear to which verse this refers.

tary of] *al-Jalālayn*[40] and others: "This does not apply in lands in which Islam is not powerful."

God, may He be glorified and exalted, said in relating the story of Joseph,[41] may God's blessing and peace be upon him: "Set me over the storehouses of the land. I am a wise custodian" (Qur'ān 12: 55). Al-Nasafī said: "...there is an indication in this that it is lawful for a man to accept a position from an unjust ruler." The elders take the place of the judiciary if it is unjustly exercised.

If the prophet or the wise man becomes aware that it is impossible to achieve government conforming to the will of God, or to remove injustice, except by giving power to the unbeliever, he must do what needs to be done.

It is clear that the sovereign acts according to his own will. One cannot object to anything that he orders, and his decisions are to be carried out. This is said by al-Bayḍāwī and other authors.

God, may He be glorified and exalted, is the only wise one.

Set down by the humble servant of God,
Sidia Ibn Muḥammad Sidia,
may God grant him forgiveness. Amen.[42]

Written on the 5th night of Shawwal,
1320 [January 5, 1903].

40. This is a Qur'ānic commentary by Jalāl al-Dīn al-Maḥallī (d. 864/1459) and Jalāl al-Dīn al-Suyūṭī (d. 911/1505).

41. The story is of relevance in this context because Joseph, whom the Islamic tradition regards as being a Muslim, was appointed as an administrator by the non-Muslim king of Egypt. The story appears in chapter (*sūra*) 12 of the Qur'ān.

42. Shaykh Sidia's fatwā was given a lengthy and approving evaluation by Sa'd Būh (d. 1917), a prominent West African cleric who was the brother of Mā' al-'Aynayn (d. 1910), the architect of a major revolt against the French. For a French translation of this approbation, see Michaux-Bellaire "Une Fetoua de Cheikh Sidia," 140-153.

– 5 –

The Birth of Minority Jurisprudence

"Minority jurisprudence" or *fiqh al-aqalliyyāt* is the name for a new branch of jurisprudence designed to meet the needs of the many millions of Muslims who now live outside the Islamic world. Today it is perhaps the fastest growing area of Islamic law. The term was coined and developed by Tahā Jābir al-ʿAlwānī (b. 1935),[1] but a major precursor of this intellectual movement was Rashīd Riḍā (d. 1354/1935), an Egyptian thinker of Levantine origin. This debt to Riḍā is frequently acknowledged by Yusūf al-Qaraḍāwī, one of the most prominent exponents of minority jurisprudence in the twenty-first century.[2] Unlike al-Alwānī and al-Qaraḍāwī, Riḍā did not identify his pronouncements on Muslims living in non-Muslim lands as being a part of a separate field of jurisprudence. However, over the course of his life, he answered dozens of questions about the issue from Muslims as far afield as China and America and a general philosophy behind these answers seems to have gradually emerged.

---

1. Biographical information on al-ʿAlwānī is based largely on the C.V. that he has posted on his website. See "C.V.", accessed July 10, 2012, http://www.alwani.net/cv.php.

2. See Umar Ryad, "A Prelude to Fiqh al-Aqaliyyât: Rashîd Ridâ's *Fatwâs* to Muslims under Non-Muslim Rule," in *In-Between Spaces: Christian and Muslim Minorities in Transition in Europe and the Middle East*, ed. Christiane Timmerman et al. (Bruxelles: Peter Lang, 2009), 241. The fatwās by Riḍā that are referenced here are also discussed by Ryad.

Riḍā was a prominent member of the Islamic reform (*iṣlāḥ*) movement developed by his teacher, Muḥammad ʿAbduh (d. 1323/1905), and Jamāl al-Dīn al-Afghānī (d. 1315/1897). The reform movement claimed that, over the centuries, Islamic thought had accrued many impurities as a result of stagnation and Islamic intellectuals' blind imitation (*taqlīd*) of the views of their predecessors. The goal of the reform movement was to return Islam to the pristine state of its early pious adherents. ʿAbduh stated his aims thus: "To liberate thought from the shackles of *taqlīd*, and understand religion as it was understood by the elders of the community before dissension appeared; to return, in the acquisition of religious knowledge, to its first sources, and to weigh them in the scales of human reason, which God has created in order to prevent excess or adulteration in religion." He stresses that "religion must be accounted a friend to science, pushing man to investigate the secrets of existence."[3] The movement performed a delicate balancing act between accommodating western modes of thought and technology, and resisting its encroachments.

Riḍā's views on Muslims living under non-Muslim rule have to be carefully pieced together from the scattered remarks that he makes on the subject over the course of responding to questions which he received from across the world. Riḍā does not rail against Muslims living outside of the abode of Islam. The basis of all of his fatwās on the subject is an acknowledgement that living in a territory ruled by non-Muslims is a fact of life for many Muslims which cannot be changed by an appeal to the obligation of migration. Migration, he says, is only obligatory under extreme circumstances where Muslims are entirely unable to observe their religion. For the most part,[4] Riḍā's accommodation of Muslims living in non-Muslim territory is not the result of a redefinition of the "abode of war." Even if Muslims have the freedom to publi-

3. Albert Hourani, *Arabic Thought in the Liberal Age, 1798-1939* (New York: Oxford University Press, 1967), 140-41.

4. In one early fatwā, Riḍā does indeed express the view that the ability to practice Islamic rituals and the presence of safety and security is enough for a land to be considered a part of the abode of Islam. See *al-Manār* 8 (8 June 1905), 291.

cally practice their religious observances, this is not enough to designate the territory an abode of Islam. An "abode of Islam" must have a Muslim ruler.[5] Thus even Syria and Lebanon under the French circa 1927, which have majority Muslim populations, are designated by Riḍā as abodes of war. His classification of non-Muslim territory as the "abode of war" does not, however, detract from his efforts to normalize life for Muslims who lived there. He relaxes several Islamic laws which might make their lives difficult. For example, he relaxes some Islamic laws of finance and the taking of interest, allows Muslims to serve in the military on the side of the Russians in the Russo-Japanese War,[6] and allows Muslims to wear European clothes.[7] Nonetheless, he does not give license to Muslims to merely capitulate to the values of the non-Muslim societies in which they live. Consider the following fatwā:

Rashīd Riḍā: On French Citizenship
(1924)[8]

[Question from the Tunisian National Party]

What does his excellency, the virtuous and great professor, the Shaykh Rashīd Riḍā, may God support him, say regarding the French government which rules over many Islamic peoples and has instituted a law known as the law of citizenship,[9] the goal of which is to bring the Muslim inhabitants of this land to leave their religion and to increase the number of factions. This citizenship has already been made a condition of receiving the political rights which they had before this and

5. *Al-Manār* 31 (4 October 1930), 273. The question is asked regarding China.
6. Ryad, "A Prelude to Fiqh al-Aqaliyyât," 242.
7. On this, see ibid., 247 ff.
8. This fatwā is translated from *al-Manār* 25 (January 1, 1924), 21-32.
9. In 1923, the French authorities in Tunisia instituted laws which made it very much easier for Tunisian Muslims to receive citizenship. On these laws and the debates concerning them, see Rudolph Peters and Gert J. J. de Vries, "Apostasy in Islam," *Die Welt des Islams* 17 (1976-77), 1-25.

of which they have been deprived by reason of the unjust tyranny. It compels a Muslim to comply with this [French] religion by making him actually refuse and deny the laws of the *Sharīʿa*, and instead follow the laws set down in texts which clearly permit fornication, partaking of alcohol, debauchery, taking interest and earning in illegal ways. They forbid polygamy and consider more than one [wife] to constitute punishable adultery. They deny the parentage of those born to [wives] other than the first, and give them no right to maintenance nor inheritance even with an avowal of paternity. They take away the husband's authority in the marriage and give authority to a court such that if he unilaterally concludes a divorce, it is ineffectual. Their division of inheritance disagrees with the obligatory *Sharīʿa* way by making portions [of inheritance] equal between males and females.

The greatest affliction of all is forcing Muslims into military service in the enemy's army which is prepared to kill Muslims, humiliate them, force them into submission and throw them into the grip of one who does not observe covenants and keep pacts. Is this government not prepared to violate the pact that has been laid down on those Muslims, tempting them in their religion and breaching the order of their society?

Are those Muslims, if they accept this citizenship, apostates in the eyes of their religion? Can they be treated as one treats Muslims in matters like marriage, inheritance, eating their meat, and burying their dead in Muslim cemeteries, given that they are content to abandon the *Sharīʿa* laws and nothing compelled them to do that? What is the position [of the *Sharīʿa*]?

Is it permissible for a Muslim, who knows the consequences of tempting the blind and the calamities of keeping silent about it, to *not* openly condemn [such behavior], if his own position is one of personal security, and he is able to resist [temptation] and to demonstrate his condemnation of it?

Give us your legal opinion on this situation regarding what

the *Sharīʿa* declares to guide the perplexed and instruct the negligent.

May God make you remain in the service of Islam and the Muslims.

[Answer]

If this situation is as you have described it in the question, there is no disagreement among the Muslims that accepting this citizenship constitutes manifest apostasy and a departure from the Islamic community. Even petitioning for a fatwā regarding it is strange in a land like Tunisia in which one would think its people would not be ignorant of the laws mentioned in the question which are, of necessity, well-known matters of religion. Perhaps the intention of seeking a fatwā is making known to the general public the meaning of this citizenship and the aforementioned matters that it entails which contradict Islam itself…

Rashīd Riḍā:
Must Muslims Leave Austro-Hungarian Bosnia?

Below is a fatwā in which Rashīd Riḍā explains why he permits Muslims to remain under non-Muslim rule in Austro-Hungarian Bosnia, provided that they are able to observe the ritual aspects of their religion. The issue of migration had long been a pressing one for Bosnian Muslims. During the war of 1737-39, the Holy Roman Emperor, Charles VI, gave the following ultimatum to Bosnian Muslims: "Whoever of them wishes to adopt Christianity may be free to stay and retain his property, while those who do not may emigrate to wherever they want."[10] Faced with this ultimatum, migrations followed. Migrations also occurred during the war of 1788-91, despite the Holy Roman Emperor Joseph II's assurance

10. Muhamed Mukafu al-Arnaut, "Islam and Muslims in Bosnia 1878-1918: Two Hijras and Two Fatwās," *Journal of Islamic Studies 5 (1994),* 246.

that he would guarantee Muslims the right to observe their religion. Then, in the nineteenth century, many Muslims migrated during the Crimean wars. Migration became so rampant that, in the 1880s, some Bosnian scholars, concerned for the future of Muslims in Bosnia, began to write against the obligation of migration.[11] While their work had some influence, it was not until Riḍā wrote his fatwā that their arguments came to be widely accepted. This is a testament to Riḍā's considerable influence and reputation, even in a land as distant from him as Bosnia.[12]

Riḍā's fatwā was published in his journal, *al-Manār*, on July 6, 1909. It was written in response to a sermon by an unnamed Ottoman visitor to Bosnia which urged Bosnian Muslims to migrate on account of non-Muslim, Austro-Hungarian rule. The Austro-Hungarians had occupied and administered Bosnia since 1878, but had allowed Bosnia to officially remain a part of the Ottoman Empire for their first three decades in power. After 1908, Bosnia became a full part of the Austro-Hungarian Empire[13] and Riḍā's treatise is written in response to this new political situation.

Rashīd Riḍā:
Must Muslims Leave Austro-Hungarian Bosnia?[14]
(1909)

From the undersigned person in Bosnia:
(The questioner is among those who are excessive in their love of *al-Manār* and its editor,[15] and he extols us with hon-

11. Ibid., 248.
12. Ibid.
13. See Fikret Karčić, *The Bosniaks and the Challenges of Modernity: Late Ottoman and Hapsburg Times* (Sarajevo: El-Kalem, 1999), 111 ff. This author also discusses other Bosnian responses to living under non-Muslim rule.
14. This fatwā is translated from *al-Manār* 12 (July 6, 1909), 410-415.
15. *Al-Manār* is the name of the journal founded in 1898 by Rashīd Riḍā in which this fatwā appears. The title means "the lighthouse" or "the beacon." The editor of *al-Manār* is, of course, Rashīd Riḍā himself.

orifics and epithets that we are abashed to mention. Nonetheless, we will publish them exactly as they came to us...)

[Question]

After greeting you, oh excellent and great master, the learned, the understanding, the magnanimous and unique, the proof of Islam, the leader of the people of truth and the glory of humankind, the scholar, the agent [of God], the virtuous, the perfect, the verifier of the truth, the noble man, the adept, the philosopher, the sage, the meticulous scholar, the cultured and intelligent man, unrivaled in this age, matchless in this epoch, our lord, master and guide, Shaykh Muḥammad Rashīd Riḍā, may God grant him a long and good life, I say:

In the name of God, the Beneficent and the Merciful. Praise God who possesses glory and magnificence, and blessings and peace on our master and lord, the delight of our eyes, His messenger who summons to the path of true religion, our master Muḥammad and also his family and his good, pure companions who were guided by him and those who followed them in excellence until the day of resurrection and recompense.

As for what follows, some of our friends informed us that one of the scholars of Astana (Kazakhstan) had agreed to deliver an admonition at the Friday prayer in one of our cities. His general point was that migration was obligatory for us and that there was an absence of legal validity for marriage and such like after Austria had seized and annexed (Bosnia and Herzegovina) for its monarch. He also stressed that there was an absence of legal validity for the pillars of Islam under its rule, including validity for prayer (and the Friday prayer is subsumed in this category), fasting, pilgrimage and almsgiving. Most of those who heard him were in a great state of confusion, thinking that the truth of the matter was in accordance with what he had said.

Oh my lord, master and delight of my eyes, oh protector

of the truth and the *Sunna*, oh subduer of abominable and despicable religious innovation, oh remover of grief from this community which is the object of [God's] mercy, oh source of emulation for the community and exemplar for the leaders, oh mercy of God for this religion of true believers, I implore your excellency to grace us with a clear and healing answer to this scholar in the manner that you have been guided by the Book and the Sunnī tradition – with proofs and powerful and satisfying legal evidence, just as your honor tirelessly accomplishes on the pages of the enlightened *al-Manār*, may God prolong its light until the Day of Resurrection and the hereafter and may He bless its owner and agent just as He treated His favorites among His God-fearing servants, and may He reward you as He rewards the righteous among His devoted servants. Truly He possesses the power to make what fitting response He wishes.

[From:] The reader of the enlightened *al-Manār*, your obedient, special friend of friends of the enlightened *al-Manār* and its editor, their lover and enemy of their enemies and haters. The weak, feeble, poor and wretched servant, the dust of the feet of the Helpers,[16] appeals to the mercy of His exalted and powerful Lord.

Muḥammad Ẓ. H. D. [Ẓahīr al-Dīn] Tārābār, a student of the Medrasa Fejzija in the city of Travnik (Bosnia).

[Answer]

There is no doubt that this Turk has erred in all that he has said. The correct view is that migration (*hijra*) is not an individual obligation for anyone who is able to maintain his religion secure from corruption (*fitna*). This corruption entails coercion to abandon it or preventing him from maintaining and performing religious duties. This is in accordance with

16. This is a reference to those residents of Medina who assisted Muḥammad upon his arrival in that town.

what ʿĀʾisha,[17] in [the *Ṣaḥīḥ*] *al-Bukhārī*, said when she was asked about [the obligation of] migration:

There is no migration today. It used to be that a believer fled with his religion to God and his Prophet in fear of being tempted [away from religion]. However today, God has made Islam victorious and the believer can serve his God wherever he wishes.[18]

As for the Qurʾānic verse, "those who are taken by the angels" (Qurʾān 4: 97), we will come to it. There are many *ḥadīth*s and scholarly opinions on [migration] and we will mention the most important of them.

[1] The *ḥadīth* which is transmitted by Ibn ʿAbbās (d. 68/687)... that the Prophet, may God bless him and grant him peace, said: "There is no migration after the conquest, but only *jihād* and intention; so if you are called [for *jihād*], offer yourself up."[19]

[2] A similar *ḥadīth* is narrated on the authority of ʿĀʾisha... that the Prophet, may God bless him and grant him peace, said: "Migration does not cease so long as the enemy is fought."[20]

This [2] agrees with the *ḥadīth* of Ibn ʿAbbās [1] on the obligation of offering oneself up when called for a *Sharīʿa*-mandated *jihād*, and of leaving one's homeland on account of that, but this obligation is not present today.

[3] As for the *ḥadīth* on the authority of Jarīr. b. ʿAbdallāh,[21] according to Abū Dāwūd and al-Tirmidhī, "I am not responsible for any Muslim who resides among the poly-

17. ʿĀʾisha bint Abī Bakr (d. 58/678) is the third and favorite wife of the Prophet according to Sunnī Muslims.

18. *Ṣaḥīḥ al-Bukhārī*, no. 4058.

19. *Ṣaḥīḥ al-Bukhārī*, no. 2783 and *Ṣaḥīḥ Muslim*, no. 1353. It is not clear what "intention" refers to in this context. It is often interpreted as the intention to wage *jihād*, that is, being in a mental state of readiness for it.

20. On this *ḥadīth*, see Crone, "The First-Century Concept of *Hiğra*," 372.

21. A chieftain of the Bajīla tribe who converted to Islam in 10/631.

theists,"[22] and his explanation of it in his words: "Their fires should not be in sight of one another" – al-Bukhārī and Abū Ḥātim [al-Rāzī] (d. 277/890) regard it as sound and include it in their collections... But this is not the same situation as that of the people of Bosnia. This is because they do not live among the polytheists…

[4] In the *ḥadīth* chapter … which we already indicated in the previous section… : "I heard the messenger of God, may God bless him and grant him peace, say: 'Neither migration nor repentance cease until the sun rises in the West.'"[23] Regarding this *ḥadīth*, al-Khaṭṭābī (d. 386/996 or 388/998)[24] said: "Its chain of authority is disputed."

As for the statements of the scholars regarding the laws [stated] in these *ḥadīth*s, we will mention what [Muḥammad b. ʿAlī] al-Shawkānī (d. 1255/1839) conveyed in his *Sharḥ al-Muntaqā*[25] on the reconciliation between them: There is disagreement regarding the reconciliation of *ḥadīth*s in this chapter.[26] Al-Khaṭṭābī and others said that migration was an obligation at the beginning of Islam for someone who converted because of the small number of Muslims in Medina and their need to gather together, but when God conquered Mecca, the people entered God's religion in droves, and the obligation of migration to Medina ceased. However, the obligation of *jihād* and intention remained for those who rose up against or who were attacked by the enemy.

Al-Ḥāfiẓ (Ibn Ḥajar al-Asqalānī [d. 852/1449]) said: "Wisdom supports the obligation of migration for one who con-

---

22. *Sunan al-Tirmidhī*, no. 1604; *Sunan Abī Dāwūd*, ed. Muḥammad Muḥyī al-Dīn ʿAbd al-Ḥamīd (Beirut: Dār al-Fikr, n.d.), no. 2645; and *Sunan al-Nasāʾī*, ed. ʿAbd al-Fattāh Abū Ghudda (Beirut: Dār al-Bashāʾir al-Islāmiyya, 1988), no. 4780.

23. See, for example, *Sunan Abī Dāwūd*, no. 2479 and *Sunan al-Nasāʾī*, no. 6711.

24. A Shāfiʿī scholar born in Bust (Sijistān), see *E.I.*,^{2} 4: 1131.

25. Published as Muḥammad ibn ʿAlī al-Shawkānī, *Nayl al-awṭār: sharḥ Muntaqā al-akhbār min aḥādith Sayyid al-Akhyār*, ed. Muḥammad Ḥallāq (Beirut: Dār Iḥyāʾ al-Turāth al-ʿArabī: Muʾassasat al-Tārīkh al-ʿArabī, 1999).

26. I.e., a reconciliation of those *ḥadīth*s which state that there is no longer an obligation of migration and those which state that the obligation of migration is permanent.

verted in order to be safe from being harmed by the unbelievers. This is because they used to punish anyone among them who converted to Islam so that he would withdraw from his religion. It was regarding them that the Qurʾānic verse came down: "As for those whom the angels take in death while they wrong themselves, [the angels] will ask: 'In what circumstances were you?' They will say: 'We were oppressed in the land.' [The angels] will say: 'Was not God's earth spacious that you could have migrated therein?'" (Qurʾān 4: 97). This verse remains the rule for someone who converts in the abode of unbelief and is able to leave it.

[Abū ʿAbdallāh] al-Māzarī (d. 536/1141) said: "If he is able to manifest religion in the land of unbelief, that land has become a part of the abode of Islam and his dwelling in it is better than traveling away from it since it is hoped that others will convert to Islam." There is no doubt that this opinion clashes with the chapter of *ḥadīth*s which imposes the prohibition against dwelling in the abode of unbelief.

Also, al-Khaṭṭābī said: "Migration to the Prophet's presence, in order to fight together with him and learn religious ordinances, was ordered when the Prophet, may God bless him and grant him peace, migrated to Medina." This is confirmed in a number of Qurʾānic verses stipulating that alliance is cut off between someone who migrates and someone who does not migrate. Thus, He said: "Those who believed but did not migrate from their homes, you have no duty to protect them until they leave their homes" (Qurʾān 8: 72). When Mecca was conquered and all the people of the tribes converted to Islam, the migration which was obligatory ceased but remained recommended.

Al-Baghawī said in *Sharḥ al-Sunna*[27]: "It is possible to understand this in a different way. Regarding his words, 'there is no migration after the conquest,' this [only] means [migra-

27. Abī Muḥammad al-Ḥusayn b. Masʿūd al-Baghawī, *Sharḥ al-sunna*, ed. ʿAlī Muḥammad Muʿawwaḍ (Beirut: Dār al-Kutub al-ʿIlmiyya, 1992).

tion] from Mecca to Medina. As for his words, 'does not cease,' this refers to the law regarding [migration] from the abode of unbelief to the abode of Islam in the case of someone who converts to Islam." He said: "It is possible to understand this in another sense. Regarding his words 'there is no migration,' this refers to [migration] towards the Prophet, may God bless him and grant him peace, wherever he might be with the intention of not returning to his homeland except with [the Prophet's] permission. As for his words, 'does not cease,' this means migration of a different kind, that of the bedouin and those like them."[28]

Ibn ʿUmar (d. 73/692) made clear the meaning … of the ceasing of migration to the Messenger of God, may God bless and grant peace to him and his family, after the conquest [of Mecca]: "Migration will not cease so long as the unbelievers are fought," which means, so long as the world has an abode of unbelief. The obligatory migration applies to someone who converts and fears corruption in his religion. It is understood that were there no abode of unbelief in the world, migration would cease because the reason for it would cease.

Ibn al-Tīn rejected the tradition that migration from Mecca to Medina was obligatory, and that one who remained in Mecca, without an excuse, was an unbeliever after the migration to Medina of the Prophet, may God bless and grant peace to him and his family. Ibn al-Ḥāfiẓ said that this rejection is not to be accepted. Ibn al-ʿArabī said: "Migration is leaving the abode of war for the abode of Islam and was obligatory according to the pact of the Prophet, may God bless and grant peace to him and his family, and continued to be so after him for someone who feared for his soul. [The migration] which truly ceased was the one with the intention of [migrating] to him [the Prophet] wherever he might be."

It is related in *al-Baḥr* that migration from the abode of

28. One of the valences of the root *h.j.r.* is to move from a nomadic to a sedentary life, see F. Donner, *The Early Islamic Conquests* (Princeton: Princeton University Press, 1981), 79 ff.

unbelief is obligatory according to consensus where disobedience is encouraged by commission or omission or where the ruler requests it by force. Jaʿfar b. Mubashshir (d. 234/848) and some of the rightly guided are of the opinion that migration is obligatory from the abode of sinfulness, by way of a syllogistic comparison with the abode of unbelief. However, this is an analogy with a discrepancy and the truth is that it is not obligatory from the abode of sinfulness because it is [still] the abode of Islam. It is clear that equating the abode of Islam with the abode of unbelief merely on account of the [presence of] sinfulness does not accord with the science of *ḥadīth* nor that of its chains of transmission. There is no basis for this position in their definitions of abodes and excuses permitting the abandonment of migration. Al-Shawkānī conveyed this and it is the quintessence of what was said in the *ḥadīth* commentaries of our scholars.

I say that you will find them differing on every aspect of the matter for two reasons. One of them is the lack of ability to maintain religion on account of the corruption (*fitna*) which entails bringing a Muslim into unbelief or opposing his religion through commission or omission, or through ignorance. The second of them is the religious war (*al-jihād al-dīnī*), that is, the one connected with protecting the call to Islam and the people's security in their religion and truth. Under these two circumstances, there is no disagreement that migration is obligatory. That is, [it is obligatory] for someone who is incapable of maintaining his religion, whether he lives alone or together with others, or for someone who is needed for a *jihād* ([that is], he has been called for duty to make the Muslims strong and aid them in the defense that is required by the *Sharīʿa*). As for this reason, it is plainly clear that it is not applicable to the people of Bosnia today, as has been submitted. Also, I do not presume to know whether the first reason applies to them, rather, they will know it for themselves...

The Turkish preacher's claims regarding the lack of legal

validity for marriage and the pillars of Islam in Bosnia after its annexation by Austria are invalid – they could not issue except from an ignoramus. If it were not for the permission of that blind imitation (*taqlīd*) which God has forbidden to the Muslims, how would this ignoramus have the means to bring doubt about their rituals and marriage contracts to those Muslims who hear his sermon?[29] If the sermon [truly] was explaining the Book of God and the *Sunna* of his Prophet, it would not have any such assertions and stupidities. But if the minds of the Muslim people become enlightened and they cling to the rope of God, then, when he [the preacher] mocks their religion, they could ask him what [proofs] he has from the Book of God and the *Sunna* of his Prophet, may God bless him and grant him peace. If he brings them, they would accept him, but if not, would they not return to him what he had brought and reject him?

With regard to ritual observance and marriage, there is no difference between [the requirements] for a Muslim living in the abode of unbelief and a Muslim living in the abode of Islam, but there are [different] rules which pertain to political, civil and military matters and some of these affect the administration of the Friday prayer. It is self-evident that migration is not as necessary and binding in any time as it was in the time of the Prophet, may God bless him and his family and grant them peace, for the purpose of assisting him and accepting his teaching. But when the polytheists intensified their harm to the Muslims before the conquest of Mecca, then, despite that, he did not respond, according to tradition, with an intensification of what the ignorant preacher proclaimed against one who did not migrate. It is reported that… the messenger of God, peace be upon him, said: "When you meet your polytheistic enemies, invite them to three courses

29. I have translated *taqlīd* as "blind imitation" in this context as this pejorative sense of the word is clearly what Riḍā intends, that is, he wishes to show that the preacher was convincing only because his listeners were habituated to blind obedience.

of action… (1) Invite them to Islam, and if they acquiesce, accept it and leave them be. (2) Then, invite them to change their abode to that of the migrants and inform them that if they do this, they will have what the migrants have, and they will be obligated in what the migrants are obligated. If they refuse to change [their abode], tell them that they will be like the bedouin Muslims. Like the believers, all of God's laws will apply to them, but they will not be entitled to any of the spoils and booty of war except if they [actually] fight along-side the Muslims. (3) If they refuse [to accept Islam], demand the poll-tax (*jizya*) from them. If they acquiesce, accept it from them and leave them be… etc."

As for what they [the jurists] said about the abode of un-belief and the abode of Islam, there is no need to expand on it here. We have previously made a study of it and one who wishes to can consult it.

– 6 –

Minority Jurisprudence in the Twentieth Century

"Minority jurisprudence" or *fiqh al-aqalliyyāt* is the name for a new branch of jurisprudence designed to meet the needs of the many millions of Muslims who now live in the West. The term was coined by Tahā Jābir al-ʿAlwānī who defines it as "a specific discipline which takes into account the relationship between the religious ruling and the conditions of the community and the location where it exists. It is a *fiqh* that applies to a specific group of people living under particular conditions with special needs that may not be appropriate for other communities."[1] Today it is perhaps the fastest growing area of Islamic law. *Fiqh al-aqalliyyāt* is characterized by considerable diversity. Due to considerations of space, however, this anthology limits itself to the work of al-ʿAlwānī. Born in Iraq in 1935, al-ʿAlwānī was educated at al-Azhar University in Egypt from which he received his doctorate in 1973.[2] Over the course of his life, al-ʿAlwānī has participated in a dizzying variety of institutions. From 1963-1979, during a particularly tumultuous period in Iraqi history which saw the rise of the Baʿth

1. Al-ʿAlwānī, *Towards a Fiqh for Minorities: Some Basic Reflections*, tr. A. Shamis (London: International Institute of Islamic Thought, 2003), 3.

2. Biographical information on al-ʿAlwānī is based on the C.V., cited above, that he has posted on his website. Cf. Ibrāhīm Salīm Abū Ḥulaywa, *Ṭāhā Jābir al-ʿAlwānī: tajalliyyāt al-tajdīd fī mashrūʿihi al-fikrī* (Beirut: Markaz al-Ḥaḍāra li-Tanmiyat al-Fikr al-Islāmī, 2011).

socialist party, al-ʿAlwānī occupied a number of Islamic educational roles in the Iraqi army. Also in Iraq, he lectured in Islamic studies at military colleges and at Islamic ones, and led a mosque. In the 1970s, he served as an advisor to the Saudi regime and was professor of Islamic law and jurisprudence at the College of Sharīʿa, University of Imām Muḥammad Ibn Saʿūd (1975-1984), the main center in Saudi Arabia for the training of Wahhābī clerics. He is thus someone who was able to simultaneously succeed in environments as different as those of the secular Arab socialism of Iraq and the religious institutions of the Saudi kingdom. After coming to the United States in 1984, he continued to involve himself in institutions with very different religious and political philosophies. He has been active in a number of Islamic organizations in the United States including the Fiqh Council of North America, the Graduate School of Islamic and Social Sciences and Cordoba University. Beginning in 1996, the Defense Department and his Graduate School of Islamic and Social Sciences set up a program to train Muslim military chaplains for the U.S. Army.[3] This partnership with the defense department has not prevented his membership in various committees of the Organization of the Islamic Conference and the Muslim World League.[4] His writings should thus be seen as an attempt to form an Islam which can withstand the pressures of an often unstable and ideologically fragmented world.

Al-ʿAlwānī is influenced by the Salafī view that a reform is necessary in order to bring Islam back to its pristine state. He has respect for the works of the jurists but nonetheless believes that, over the centuries, they have added accretions to Islam that render it unnecessarily rigid. He says that the jurisprudence of the past, although "varied and rich… was closely associated with the historical circumstances in which it was developed." Therefore, he

3. Phillip Kurata, "Bangladeshi American is First Muslim Chaplain in Marine Corps: Abuhena Saifulislam Counsels Troops from all Backgrounds and Faiths," published February 4, 2008, accessed July 10, 2012, http://www.america.gov/st/diversity-english/2008/February/20080204123903cpataruk0.6934015.html.

4. Based in Saudi Arabia, the Muslim World League is one of the largest Islamic nongovernmental organizations.

says, it "is part of its own time and space and none of it can be applied to other substantially different situations."[5] It can only be used as non-binding precedent which can be used as a "guide." To counteract those who treat Islamic jurisprudence as something more binding, he speaks of the need for a return to the ideals of the Qurʾān and the *ḥadīth* and of the need for *ijtihād* (independent judicial thought). This *ijtihād* will be applied in a spirit of "ease and mercy"[6] because, he says, "*Sharīʿah* laws are based on clemency and temperance rather than oppression and severity... Permissibility is the norm." Al-ʿAlwānī acknowledges that some of the laws developed as a part of this new branch of jurisprudence will contradict established Islamic laws. While he believes that conflict should be minimized, he justifies contradicting previous laws on the grounds of judicial "necessity." The necessity is the product of two related factors. The first is the need to aid Muslims as they proselytize and expand Islam in the West. The second is that of preventing Muslim minorities from making their own rules and, in so doing, deviating from Islam.[7]

Al-ʿAlwānī applies his principle of flexibility to minority jurisprudence itself. He says that the laws that are developed should not themselves become a cause of the calcification of the Islamic tradition. Muslims, he says, should always have the opportunity to reconsider these new laws as their needs change over time. His desire is for Islamic law to be something that is fluid and easily adaptable. As a result of this philosophy, al-ʿAlwānī is able to give legal opinions which many have regarded as contradicting generally accepted Islamic opinions. Thus, for example, he regards the visual representation of the Prophet Muḥammad in a United States Supreme Court frieze as permissible, and even as a compliment to the Muslims,[8] and he gives his approval of a fatwā which permits

5. al-ʿAlwānī, *Towards a Fiqh for Minorities*, 7.

6. al-ʿAlwānī, *Issues in Contemporary Islamic Thought* (Herndon: International Institute of Islamic Thought, 2005), 134.

7. On this, see al-ʿAlwānī, "al-Gharb fī al-muslimīn istīṭān baʿd al-Islām tawṭīn," *al-Sharq al-Awsāṭ*, 18 January 2000, accessed July 19, 2012, http://web.archive.org/web/20050107010951/http://www.alhramain.com/text/alraseed/958/qazaya/2.htm.

8. al-ʿAlwānī, "'Fatwa' concerning the United States Supreme Courtroom Frieze," *Journal of Law and Religion* 15 (2000-2001), 1-28.

Muslims to fight in the U.S. military against other Muslims.[9] In both of these fatwās, al-ʿAlwānī's aim is to make Islam easier to observe in the American environment. Below is an example of a fatwā by al-ʿAlwānī on the question of whether Muslims can participate in the American political system.

Al-ʿAlwānī: On Participation in the American Political Process

(2000)[10]

December 8, 2000.
American Muslim Council: Towards the Political Empowerment of Muslims in America

In the Name of Allah, the Most Gracious, Most Merciful

Fatwa Concerning the Participation of Muslims in the American Political Process

By Dr. Taha Jaber al-ʿAlwani
Chairman of the North American *Fiqh* Council
President of the Graduate School of Social and Islamic Sciences

We have received from the American Muslim Council the following inquiry:

[Inquiry]

You know that the American Muslim Council is in the midst of a voting registration campaign for the forthcoming

9. Basheer Nafi, "Fatwā and War: On the Allegiance of the American Muslim Soldiers in the Aftermath of September 11," *Islamic Law and Society* 11 (2004), 78-116.

10. This unmodified, English-language text is from the Internet Archive, accessed June 5, 2012, http://web.archive. org/web/20001208111/http://www.amconline.org/newamc/fatwa.shtml. It is reproduced here with the kind permission of the author.

American elections. In the course of this campaign, some American Muslims have expressed severe doubts as to whether it would be religiously permissible for them to participate in the political system of this country, the United States of America. Several reasons were cited for this doubt.

Some argue that participation would ally some Muslims with others they have little in common with in matters of belief. It may also divide Muslims in the United States, and harm the interests of the Muslim community. This would be in contradiction to the Qur'anic injunction that Muslims should support each other.

Others argue that participation in our system may be viewed as *rukun* (acquiescence) to the unjust. The Almighty said in the Qur'an: "And do not acquiesce to the unjust…"

Yet others argue that the participation of Muslims in our secular political system, which is increasingly denuding the public square from all symbols of faith, would desensitize Muslims into accepting the current status-quo and interacting with it, to the detriment of all people of faith in this society.

Additionally, some Muslims, who escaped dictatorial regimes in their countries of origin or left to avoid bad economic conditions, live in the hope of going back to Dar al-Islam (Land of Islam) once the situation improves. This state of affairs is not uncommon among first generation immigrants, Muslim or otherwise. In our case, however, we are concerned about the fact that it leads to voting apathy. In particular, some Muslims in this group argue that voting can be justified only for extreme necessity.

We would like your Eminence to clarify this matter for us with a lucid statement which, with proofs and arguments, may bring to an end the conflict among American Muslims over this vital issue.

May Allah reward you with His blessings.

Aly Ramadan Abuzaakouk
Executive-Director of the American Muslim Council

[Reply]

In an independent research entitled "Introduction to Minorities Jurisprudence: Founding Views" (the "Introduction"), to be published this fall in a special issue on Islam by the *Journal of Law & Religion*,[11] we dealt with the principles and rules that should govern the vision of the contemporary jurist (and the contemporary Muslim in general) on this topic. The connection of this *fatwa* to the *Introduction* is akin to that of a derivative principle (a branch) to a fundamental principle (a root), or of an example to the general rule. The understanding, therefore, of the *Introduction* and the orthodoxy of prevailing principles and argumentation contained therein, is necessary for a better understanding of this *fatwa* and the foundation on which it rests.

Overview of Basic Principles:

Among the legal and methodological principles we reached in the *Introduction* are the following:

1. All of humankind is one family that belongs in its entirety to Adam, and Adam is from earth. This humanity is divided into two nations: "A nation that responds" and "a nation that summons."[12]
2. Islam is a global religion, not restricted to any one ethnic group or geographical area.
3. The Qur'anic discourse is global and should not be restricted to a limited geographical place or a narrow social group.
4. The Muslim *ummah*[13] is a benevolent one that evolved to bear witness to humanity.

11. To date, the article does not seem to have been published in the *Journal of Law and Religion*.

12. I.e., the world is divided into those who are Muslims and those who are not yet Muslims. Those who are Muslims are expected to invite those who are not Muslims to Islam.

13. The Arabic word for "nation" or "community."

5. The principle of "righteousness and equity," mentioned in the Holy Qur'an, is the greatest general principle by which to measure the relationship between Muslims and others. All other matters should concede to this principle.
6. We should avoid being limited by juristic terminologies regarding the issue of international partitions. Terms, such as "Dar al-Islam" (The Land of Islam), were not mentioned in the Revelation in the geographical sense. They are but juristic and administrative terms, the use of which was imposed by the circumstances of the old science and the nature of relationships among countries, nations and peoples at that time.
7. To properly understand the particular examples found in the inherited body of jurisprudence, they should be examined in light of the general principles mentioned herein. By so doing, we can transcend the particulars and merge them into the general principles of the Qur'an, namely, its universal message and goals.
8. The existence of Islam in any country which is not part of the original Muslim World, should be viewed as a new and developing existence which falls in harmony with the universality of Islam and its message of hope.
9. The nature of contemporary international realities, which are characterized by both the interrelation and transcendence of borders, should be taken into serious consideration.
10. Current international legal instruments and domestic laws, which address human rights and civil rights, should be relied upon to protect and educate Muslim minorities. For example, Article 21 of the International Declaration of Human Rights states that each individual has the right to participate in the administration of his or her own country's public affairs, whether directly or via representatives.
11. The principles of justice included in such documents should be followed as they are in harmony with the sermon of the Messenger (Peace be upon him) to his followers at

his Farewell Pilgrimage[14] and to "the alliance" which he attended at Ibn Jud'an's house.[15] In addition, all legitimate means, including political participation, should be utilized to safeguard these principles of justice.

12. The lessons derived from the early Islamic experience, in particular the emigration to Ethiopia,[16] should be fully understood.
13. There should be a transition from negative reasoning about what is permissible to positive reasoning in carrying the Message to the people of our society.

American Particularities:

America has particularities that need to be considered in order to issue the most appropriate legal ruling. Among these particularities are:

1. The United States is a country of immigrants who are of different races and various cultures. It is not wholly identified by any one people or immigrant culture. In particular, American culture does not exclude non-Europeans.
2. The United States is a young country whose civilization and culture have an open nature, unlike ancient civiliza-

14. There are many versions of the Prophet's farewell sermon. On this, see A. Hakim, "Conflicting Images of Lawgivers: The Caliph and the Prophet: *Sunnat ʿUmar* and *Sunnat Muḥammad*," in *Method and Theory in the Study of Islamic Origins*, ed. H. Berg (Brill: Leiden, 2003), 161 ff.

15. This refers to the famous pact known as the *ḥilf al-fuḍūl* in which Muḥammad participated several years before his prophetic mission. There are many versions of what exactly occurred, but the pact seems to have been the result of a commercial transaction which went wrong and caused strife between a number of clans. The content of the pact is summarized by C. Pellat: "The participants swore to be 'like a single hand with the oppressed and against the oppressor,' to have justice done to all victims whatever their origin and their situation and to afford mutual aid and assistance." The importance of this arrangement for al-ʿAlwānī is that Muḥammad agreed to it before he received revelation and confirmed it again after he received revelation. For Pellat on the pact, see *Encyclopedia of Islam*, 2nd ed., s.v., "Ḥilf al-Fuḍūl."

16. The author is referring to an event in which several early Muslims fled persecution in Mecca for asylum in Abyssinia between 614-615. This migration was made in advance of the Prophet's migration to Medina in 622. For an outline of the migration to Abyssinia, see Montgomery Watt, *Muḥammad at Mecca* (Oxford: Oxford University Press, 1953), 115 ff.

tions that tend to have definitively established characteristics. This makes the American culture more open to the contributions of Islam and Muslims.

3. The United States is a country of freedom that looks primarily after the rights of all of its citizens, of all religions and races, despite the problems in application that manifest themselves from time to time.
4. The United States has peoples among whom racism is relatively less manifested due to their intellectual background and the historical experience of its Protestant majority.

Based on these principles and particularities, we can deduce the following conclusions with respect to the participation of Muslims in American political life:

Conclusions:

First, it is the duty of American Muslims to participate constructively in the political process, if only to protect their rights, and give support to views and causes they favor. Their participation may also improve the quality of information disseminated about Islam. We call this participation a "duty" because we do not consider it merely a "right" that can be abandoned or a "permission" which can be ignored. It falls into the category of safeguarding of necessities and ensuring the betterment of the Muslim community in this country.

Second, every legitimate means or tool that helps achieve these noble goals is similarly judged. This includes:

1. The nomination of any competent American Muslim for election to any post where his or her presence may ensure either bringing benefits to American Muslims and other citizens or preventing harm to them. These posts range from those of mayor, state governor, and membership in educational and municipal councils, all the way up to membership in the U.S. Senate and House of Representatives.

2. Self-candidacy by an American Muslim, if the initiative for his/her nomination is not undertaken by the community, or if election laws require this form of candidacy. (Refer to the statement by Ibn Hajr[17] on the question of becoming an amir (or coming into power) in the *Introduction*.)
3. Adopting a non-Muslim candidate if he/she would be either more beneficial or less harmful to the American Muslim community and the rest of the country.
4. Providing financial support to a non-Muslim candidate. God the Almighty has permitted righteous conduct and good relations with non-Muslims in exchange for nothing. So how much more so is such support permitted if clear and tangible benefits were to result from such behavior?
5. Obtaining American citizenship. Such citizenship emphasizes the true diversity of this country and is a necessary condition for participation in the political process.
6. Both registering to vote and participation in elections and voting are means to a goal. Hence, they are subject to the same legal ruling as their intended goal.

Limitations and Specifications:

1. Protection of Muslim civil rights in this country and the enjoyment of positive interaction with other Americans requires American Muslims to engage in acts of deliberation to reach consensus on general principles, and to tolerate disagreement on particulars and disputed matters. We find a good example to follow in our ancestors who migrated to Ethiopia. They met and deliberated together about the best way to respond to the critical situation they faced.
2. The children of the Muslim minority must have a fair opportunity to develop and deepen their faith in God and Islam. Otherwise, their interaction with others may lead them to compromise on the basic tenets of their religion

17. I.e., Ibn Ḥajar al-Asqalānī (d. 852/1449).

merely to keep up with a prevailing custom or sweeping current. Ja'far, by refusing to bow to al Najashi –The King of Abyssinia– (his two Quraishi opponents did as necessitated by custom) provides a good example for such situations.

3. The Muslim minority needs to have a fair opportunity to express clearly in its own voice the immortal truths of Islam and its advanced system of human values. The example of Ja'far helps in this regards. In his eloquent speech to al Najashi, Ja'far summarized the main Islamic virtues and explained the difference between them and those of the pre-Islamic life (the Jahiliyah). By applying this method, Muslims not only gain the understanding of the rest of the people, but also their good will.
4. Both the art of persuasion and the science of public relations have an important role that should not be ignored. The words by which Ja'far ended his speech are appropriate here: "We came out to your country, we chose you from all others, we wished to be in your neighborhood, and hoped, O King, not to be treated unjustly in your country".

Objections:

As for the objections mentioned in the inquiry and raised by some of our brothers and sisters, they can be summarized in five points which are discussed as follows:

The First Argument:

Participation would ally some Muslims with others they have little in common with in matters of belief. It may also divide Muslims in the United States and harm the interests of the Muslim community. This would be in contradiction to the Qur'anic injunction that Muslims should support each other.

This argument is based on an incorrect presumption resulting from two errors:

First, the argument casts pragmatic considerations as matters of belief, although there is a vast difference between the two. The fair dealing of Muslims with others and their cooperation with them produce neither blind allegiance (*wala'*) to these others nor special exceptions (*bara'*) for them. For this is not originally a matter of belief but is instead a pragmatic decision involving the proper implementation of the principles of "righteousness," "fairness and equity," success and constructive behavior.

Second, the argument confuses the limited meaning of the concept of "alliance" (*wala'*) referred to in the Qur'an, with a broader all-inclusive one. The type of alliance warned against in the Qur'an is that which harms the interests of the Muslim community. This meaning is mentioned repeatedly in the Qur'an in such a way as to leave no confusion.

The Almighty, threatening the hypocrites, said: "To the hypocrites give the glad tidings that there is for them (but) a grievous penalty. Yea, to those who take for *'awlia'* (allies) unbelievers (those who do not believe in God) rather than believers." (Qur'an 4: 138-139). He then warned the believers: "O you who believe! Take not for *awliya'* unbelievers rather than believers." (Qur'an: 4: 144). Confirming the warning in another verse, the Almighty said: "Let not the Believers take for *awliya'* Unbelievers rather than Believers."(Qur'an: 3: 28).

But the meaning of specific Qur'anic verses is determined by various factors, including the context, reasons for revelation, other verses related to them, and even the *sunnah* of the Prophet (Peace be upon him). For example, we know that the Prophet befriended the Christian Ethiopian king al Najashi.[18] We also know that the Prophet executed an alliance with the Jews of Madinah giving them rights similar to those of

18. On al-Najāshī, a figure famous for giving refuge to some of Muḥammad's early followers before the migration to Medina, see *Encyclopedia of Islam*, 2nd ed., s.v., "al-Nadjāshī."

Muslims.[19] Most importantly, we know that the Qur'an refers to Christians and Jews as "People of the Book," and not as "Unbelievers." So, even if the meanings of certain words are construed broadly, the above-cited Qur'anic verses do not prohibit Muslims from building alliances with the vast majority of Americans.

But to gain insight into the proper interpretation of the Qur'anic verses, it is important to examine the explanation provided by major scholars. In interpreting these Qur'anic verses, al Tabari said: "This is a prohibition from God to his servants the believers against acting like the hypocrites who take for *awliya'* unbelievers rather than the believers even where such behavior harms the interests of the community" (*Tafsir al-Tabari*, vol. 9: 336). Al Tabari added that the verse means that believers should not take the unbelievers as back-up support and partisans against their own community, showing them the vulnerabilities of the Believers" (*Tafsir al-Tabari*, vol. 6: 303).

As stated in these Qur'anic verses, then, the blameworthy alliance is that which is given to support those who do not believe in God against the interest of one's own believing community. This is a far cry from the actions of those who cooperate with non-Muslims (believers as well as unbelievers) within the limits of "righteousness and equity" while continuing to work for the good of the Muslim community.

The Second Argument:

Political participation is a type of *rukun* (acquiescence) to those who do wrong. This is prohibited by the Qur'an where the Almighty warns against such acts by His words: "And do not acquiesce to the unjust …" (Qur'an: 11:113).

---

19. Al-ʿAlwānī is referring to the "Constitution of Medina" which says that while the Jews "have their religion and the Muslims have theirs," the Jews are said to constitute "one community with the believers." The literature on this document is very extensive. Much of it is referred to in Michael Lecker, *The 'Constitution of Medina': Muhammad's First Legal Document* (Princeton: The Darwin Press, 2004).

It is wrong to understand *rukun*, as used in the above verse, to include all types of cooperation. There is no evidence for that. *Rukun* in fact means "to acquiesce to the unjust" or "to be satisfied with their doings" or "to return to idolatry." These three meanings were derived by Al Tabari from the *salaf* (the worthy ancestors) (*Tafsir al Tabari,* vol. 15: 500-501). Again, these meanings are a far cry from an act of participation intent on promoting public interest and protecting the Muslim minority from injustice.

The Third Argument:

Participation of Muslims in our political system is an acceptance of the secular (i.e., faithless, non-believing) status quo.

This argument is based on [a] misunderstanding of the American system, as well as faulty logic.

First, the framers of our American system did not intend it to be "faithless" or "non-believing," but rather faith-neutral. Ideally, our political system is not intended to oppose religious values but to be unaligned with those of any one sect or religion.

Second, passivity and withdrawal from life are what brings about acceptance of the status quo by deed, which is far more effective than words. Positive participation, on the other hand, is what showcases Islamic values and morals to civil society. Indeed, it is what refutes any "faithless" secular status quo by offering people an illustration of the blessings of faith.

The Fourth Argument:

Participation of Muslims in our secular political system, which is increasingly denuding the public square from all symbols of faith, would desensitize Muslims into accepting the current status-quo and interacting with it, to the detriment of all people of faith in this society.

Methodologically, this argument contains two errors:

First, it transfers a conceptual confusion that occurs in countries that have Muslim majorities to countries where Muslims are a minority. The two contexts are quite different and entail different obligations. While Muslims in Muslim countries are obligated to uphold the Islamic law of their state, Muslim minorities in the United States are not required either by Islamic law or rationality to uphold Islamic symbols of faith in a secular state, except to the extent permissible within that state.

What is required of Muslim minorities in a secular society is the support of the Islamic existence of their community and the service of public interest through serious participation in public life. They are also required to work hard towards building a coherent, stable and flourishing Islamic community capable of properly representing Islam to the majority, and building bridges with other faith communities. Only then can the discussion of the place of faith within our secular society become possible.

Such was the methodology of the Prophets (Peace be upon them), and such was that of our Prophet (Peace be upon him) who began by building first the Islamic community, then the Islamic society, and then the Islamic system.

Second, this argument narrows the scope of participation to the political sense. It would be more precise to consider each contribution towards enhancing the values of truth, goodness, and justice as a brick in the construction of a fair and equitable system. If the Muslim minority, through its positive participation in the making or influencing of political decisions manages to promulgate a law against the use of drugs, for example, then it would have promoted the values of truth and goodness shared by many. This is in accord with Islamic values that require Muslims to serve their communities.

The Fifth Argument:

Participation contradicts the intent of a temporary stay in this country and an eventual return to Dar al Islam (the Land of Islam).

This argument is based on historical perspectives and outdated juristic terms, such as "Dar al Islam" (The Land of Islam) and "Dar al Kufr" (The Land of Disbelief) or "Dar al Islam" and "Dar al Harb" (The Land of War). We have shown in the *Introduction* that these terms stand on a weak foundation from a legal perspective and are not applicable to contemporary international realities whether from a realistic perspective or a *manaati* one (one based on the underlying cause upon which the legal ruling *hukm* hangs. Refer to the *Introduction* for further explanation).

We can also add here that this argument ignores the highly significant fact that Islam established its first society in a land of immigration, namely, "Al Madinah al Munawwarah,"[20] and not in the original land of the Message ("Makkah al Mukarramah").[21] The Prophet (Peace be upon him) did not agree to move to Makkah after his enemies lost their battles of aggression against him. He held on to the land of his immigration, and addressed its people who gave him support and victory, saying: "To live is to live with you and to die is to die with you."

20. I.e., Medina the Illuminated.
21. I.e., Mecca the Blessed.

Against Minority Jurisprudence – The Views of Saʿīd Ramaḍān al-Būṭī

Saʿīd Ramaḍān al-Būṭī (d. 2013) was a professor of Islamic law, prolific author and media personality who, from the late 1970s, came to have close ties with the Syrian regime.[22] He was born in Turkey to a family of ethnic Kurds who then fled Turkey as a result of Ataturk's secularizing reforms. In Islamic legal circles, he is known for his traditional approach to Islamic legal sources. Despite affirming the need for *ijtihād* (independent judicial thinking) in matters which are not yet ruled upon by the law, he is at pains to locate most judicial thinking within the confines of textual sources. He thus criticizes those modernists who "believe that *ijtihād* is a kind of secret recipe to fulfill all their dreams, to open all gates and to pull down all barriers, a kind of permission to do forbidden things."[23]

Given his conservative approach to Islamic law, it is not surprising that al-Būṭī has condemned "minority jurisprudence" (*fiqh al-aqalliyyāt*) in the strongest terms, targeting both al-Alwānī personally and the European Council of Fatwā and Research, directed by Yusūf al-Qaraḍāwī, which is the most active organization promoting this branch of law. His argument is that what changes from region to region is not Islamic law itself, but only the ability of a Muslim to fulfill it. It is therefore not appropriate to restructure Islamic law because Muslims live under different social and political circumstances. He says that "minority jurisprudence" is a product of pressure on Muslims by Western politicians to assimilate to the societies in which they live and he does not feel that Muslims should succumb to these pressures. He says that the main result of modifying Islamic law to fit these circumstances will be the fragmentation of Islam. Although he does not think that Western Europe and the United States are abodes of war, he says that they

22. For al-Būṭī's biography, I have relied on Andreas Christmann, "Islamic Scholar and Religious Leader: Shaikh Muḥammad Saʿid Ramadan al-Buti," in *Islam and Modernity: Muslim Intellectuals Respond*, J. Cooper et al. (London: I. B. Tauris, 1998), 57-81.
23. Ibid., 68.

are still abodes of unbelief and that it is therefore undesirable for Muslims to live permanently in them.[24] Muslims may, however, reside there temporarily for the purpose of study, work or proselytism.[25]

Al-Būṭī: It is No Coincidence: The Convergence Between the Call for Minority Jurisprudence and the Plan for the Fragmentation of Islam[26]
(2001)

At a time in the world when the leaders of the intellectual invasion plot to fragment the unified global Islam into multiple regional Islams, which would then differ and conflict; [at a time of] growing and continuous voices calling for the creation of what they call "minority jurisprudence" (*fiqh al-aqalliyyāt*) and its elaboration of an Islamic attire fitting for an Islam which is increasing today in the West, in Europe and America, disregarding the other Islam which has in general prevailed in Islamic countries, I ask, what legal evidence or basis is there which would warrant this "minority jurisprudence" to be generated?

It has been said to me: There is much [legal evidence]: The principle of communal welfare (*maṣāliḥ*)..., necessities permit prohibited things..., difficulty brings about ease..., He

24. Al-Būṭī's most extensive statement of his views on minority jurisprudence is contained in his lecture on the subject at the Islamic University of Rotterdam (March 23, 2007), see "Fiqh al-aqalliyyāt," accessed July 12, 2012), http://www.iurtv.nl/ar/58/Prof.%20Dr.%20Buti.htm.

25. Zekeriya Budak, "Al-Bouti's Attitude Towards Fiqh al-Aqalliyyât: Islamic Jurisprudence for Muslim Minorities in Non Islamic Societies" (M.A. Thesis: University of Leiden, 2011), 19.

26. Taken from al-Būṭī, "Monthly Word June 2001," posted August 18, 2001, accessed June 11, 2012, http://web.archive.org/web/20010818021859/http://www. bouti.com/ulamaa/bouti/bouti_monthly15.htm, accessed 6/11/2012.

does not appoint for you any distress in religion.[27]

I say: But this legal evidence is not specific to Muslims living in Europe and America... It is legal evidence for a global Islamic jurisprudence which is not limited to a [particular] homeland, and there has never been legal evidence for what you call "minority jurisprudence." Wherever urgent need (*ḍarūra*) is encountered according to its accepted definition in the *Sharīʿa*, the [legal] prohibition which causes it is removed. Wherever difficulty is encountered that exceeds the usual limit, the *Sharīʿa*'s obligatory leniency is enacted to remove it and, where two concerns for communal welfare conflict in the hierarchy of the aims of the *Sharīʿa*, the more fundamental of them takes precedence.[28] We do not find in the Qurʾān, the *Sunna* or the discourses of the leading Islamic legal authorities, that this legal evidence is specific to the condition of minorities who live in the abodes of unbelief, and that it is not permissible for other Muslims in the world to use and rely upon it.

It was said to me: The urgent need which necessitates a jurisprudence specific to these minorities stems from their presence in non-Islamic societies that have special characteristics which differentiate them from Islamic societies.

I say: Which Islam is it that declares, merely on account of the presence of a Muslim in the abode of unbelief, that there is an urgent need which justifies the legislation of an Islamic jurisprudence specific to it and which is in line with the currents of unbelief, sin and disobedience which surround it?! Did God not enact and order migration (*hijra*) from the abode of unbelief to the abode of Islam for a Muslim there

27. These are all legal maxims which stipulate that it is permissible to cancel (usually only temporarily) Islamic laws which have an adverse effect on the lives of Muslims. On these maxims, see Wolfhart Heinrichs, "Qawāʿid as a Genre of Legal Literature," in *Studies in Islamic Legal Theory*, ed. Bernard Weiss (Leiden: Brill, 2002), 365-76 and Intisar Rabb, "Doubt's Benefit: Legal Maxims in Islamic Law, 7th-16th Centuries" (Ph.D. Dissertation: Princeton University, 2009).

28. On conflicts between different types of communal welfare, see Felicitas Opwis, *Maṣlaḥa and the Purpose of the Law* (Leiden: Brill, 2010), 78.

who was not permitted to apply the laws of Islam? Did the Messenger of God and his companions remain among the polytheists in Mecca? Is there not legal evidence in this that he [the Prophet] did not acknowledge what they call "minority jurisprudence"?

If the mere presence of Muslims in the abode of unbelief was a source for the [legal category of] urgent need which justifies creating a new jurisprudence to suit the situation of that abode and those who are in it, then who are those whom God, may He be exalted, intends in his words?:

"As for those whom the angels take in death while they wrong themselves, [the angels] will ask: 'In what circumstances were you?' They will say: 'We were oppressed in the land.' [The angels] will say: 'Was not God's earth spacious that you could have migrated therein?' As for these, their abode will be hell, an evil journey's end" (Qur'ān 4: 97).

We had rejoiced at the prospect that the increase of Muslims in the West, with their commitment to Islam and their upholding of its laws, would bring about the dissolution of the sinful Western civilization in the currents of Islamic civilization. However today, in the shadow of the persistent call for the so-called "minority jurisprudence," we learn that we are, on the contrary, threatened by what we had rejoiced in. We are threatened by the dissolution of Islamic existence in the currents of sinful western civilization – with a guarantee provided by this jurisprudence.

Should not the leaders of this movement – which was unheard of before today – fear God and realize that what it will produce will be the actualization of that which threatens to befall Islam today, that is, its transformation into multiple regional and diverse Islams?! We in the many legal academies in our Arabic and Islamic world have no need for the invention of special authorities who specialize in this new Islamic jurisprudence which the Islamic *Sharīʿa* does not acknowledge.

– Appendix –

Israel/Palestine

As a result of the Arab-Israeli war of 1967, Muslim populations in East Jerusalem, the West Bank, Gaza, and the Golan Heights came under Israeli rule. The question thus arose in Islamic legal circles as to whether Muslims could remain under the rule of this non-Muslim state. Perhaps the most famous discussion of it was between the scholars Muḥammad Nāṣir al-Dīn al-Albānī (d. 1420/1999) and Saʿīd Ramaḍān al-Būṭī (whom we have already encountered).

Al-Albānī was a complex figure.[1] He was born in Albania but spent most of his life in Syria and Saudi Arabia. He was deeply influenced by the reformist writings of Rashīd Riḍā which advocated a return to an early age of Islam, purified from the later accretions of the jurists. However, unlike Riḍā, al-Albānī was very distrustful of using unaided human reason to formulate the law and instead advocated an approach to jurisprudence which focused more heavily on the study and analysis of *ḥadīth*. There is a strong anti-political current in al-Albānī's thought. He was distrustful of the Muslim Brotherhood[2] because he claimed that they valued politics over religion. He famously opined that a good policy to live by is to avoid politics (*min al-siyāsa tark al-siyāsa*).[3] This being said,

1. On al-Albānī, see Stéphane Lacroix, "Between Revolution and Apoliticism: Nasir al-Din al-Albani and his Impact on the Shaping of Contemporary Salafism," in *Global Salafism: Islam's New Religious Movement* (New York: Columbia University Press, 2009), 58-80.

2. The Muslim Brotherhood is commonly considered to be the first Islamist organization. The classic work on the development of the Brotherhood is Richard Mitchell, *The Society of the Muslim Brothers* (London: Oxford University Press, 1969).

3. Ibid., 69.

the non-establishment nature of al-Albānī's views and his strident manner of expressing them led him into frequent conflicts with the authorities, leading on one occasion to his expulsion from Saudi Arabia and his imprisonment in Syria. Thus, perhaps paradoxically, his thought is viewed by many to have had a profound political impact. Al-Albānī's principle, however, of shunning the realm of politics is dramatically illustrated in his statement, translated below, on whether Muslims can remain in territories occupied by Israel after the 1967 war. He views the situation as one in which the goal of maintaining territory is in conflict with the goal of observing Islam. He argues that the value of observing Islam is of greater importance and concludes that remaining in non-Muslim territory violates Islamic law. He thus mandates migration even if it results in the loss of territory and in Muslims suffering hardship. It should be noted that al-Albānī's position on migration could well have been influenced by his own personal experience. As a child, his father decided that the secularizing reforms of Ahmet Zogu's government had rendered Albania an abode of war and concluded that migration (*hijra*) from Albania had become obligatory. The result was that, in the mid-1920s, the family migrated to Damascus.[4] Thus al-Albānī may have viewed what he asked of Palestinian Muslims as nothing more than what his family had already sacrificed.

4. Muḥammad b. Ibrāhīm al-Shaybānī, *Ḥayāt al-Albānī wa-āthāruhu wa-thanāʾ al-ʿulamāʾ ʿalayhi* (Hawalli: al-Dār al-Salafiyya, 1987), 44.

Al-Albānī: On Remaining in Territories Occupied by Israel

(late twentieth century)[5]

[Question]

Regarding the migration (*hijra*) of the people of the West Bank to another Muslim country…. Does this migration have a relation to the *ḥadīth* which says: "There is no migration after the conquest [of Mecca]."[6]

[Answer]

No, there is no relation. Regarding the legal meaning of the *ḥadīth*, "there is no migration after the conquest" – the intention is not to absolutely reject migration from the lands of the unbeliever to the lands of Islam. Rather, the intention is to deny the obligation of migration from Mecca to Medina. This is because, at the beginning of Islam, there was an obligation for the weak and oppressed Muslims of Mecca to migrate from Mecca to Medina after the Prophet, may God bless him and grant him peace, had founded the basis of the Muslim state there. Once the situation of the Prophet, may God bless him and grant him peace, had stabilized and Islam had begun to take root and gain strength in the land, [the Prophet], peace be upon him, said: "There is no migration after the conquest of Mecca."

As for migration of the general kind, it does not cease. It is among the inherited doctrines of the Muslims, which are mentioned in the books of doctrines, that [the obligation of] migration is to be performed until the Day of Resurrection.

As for the Qur'ānic text: "Was not God's earth spacious

5. This fatwā is translated from ʿUkāshah ʿAbd al-Mannān al-Ṭībī, *Fatāwā al-shaykh al-Albānī wa-muqāranatuhā bi-fatāwā al-ʿulamāʾ* (Cairo: Maktabat al-Turāth al-Islāmī, 1994), 18. Most of al-Albānī's fatwās were given orally, circulated on audiocassettes, and sometimes transcribed like this one and the other one below. It is unfortunate that no date appears on either of these fatwās.

6. *Ṣaḥīḥ al-Bukhārī*, no. 2783 and *Ṣaḥīḥ Muslim*, no. 1353.

that you could have migrated therein?" (Qurʾān 4: 97). This Qurʾānic text is decisive, firmly established and has not been abrogated. As for the *ḥadīth*, [its application] is restricted to the Qurʾānic text and to a specific time as I have elucidated above. There is therefore no contradiction.

[Question]

Is it permissible for the people of the West Bank to leave and migrate to another land?

[Answer]

It is obligatory for them to leave… Oh my brother, it is obligatory for them to leave a land in which they have no power to expel the unbeliever for a land in which it they are able to establish the Islamic observances (*shaʿāʾir al-Islāmiyya*)…

* * *

Another Fatwā by Al-Albānī[7]

[Question]

What obligation is incumbent upon the people of Palestine of today? What is the law of the abode in which they live?

[Answer]

He [al-Albānī] said: One who is able to migrate to an Islamic country, escaping with his religion and his life, is obligated to do so. As for one who is not able, he must be patient as the weak were at the beginning of the Islamic era. This is obligatory for each person who is there.

As for the law of the abode in which they live, it is an abode under the laws of unbelief. If there are Muslims living there, it is obligatory for them to kill the Jewish usurpers until

7. Nawwāf Hāyil Takrūrī, *Aḥkām al-taʿāmul al-siyāsī maʿa al-Yahūd fī Filasṭīn al-muḥtalla* (Damascus: Dār al-Shihāb, 2000), 595. This fatwā is also undated.

the land is returned to its Muslim people.

Al-Būṭī: A Refutation of Nāṣir al-Dīn al-Albānī on Palestine
(1993, republished in 1997)[8]

A few months ago, Nāṣir al-Dīn al-Albānī shocked the people with a strange fatwā which greatly deviates from the laws of the Islamic *Sharīʿa* and entirely contradicts the foundations and principles of religion. He publicly declared in the presence of witnesses that Muslims present in occupied lands, including the remaining Palestinians, are all obligated to emigrate and leave the land to the Jews who, after occupying it, transformed it into an abode of unbelief (according to his assertion)! Were it not for the frequent reports of this and were it not for the audio cassettes which played these words in the voice of the shaykh [al-Albānī], I would have been unable to believe it! This is because [even] the most unsophisticated student of the *Sharīʿa* knows that, as is established in all the sources of Islamic law, the abode of Islam legally remains the abode of Islam until the Day of Resurrection regardless of whether the unbeliever causes corruption in it. And it is an obligation for Muslims to assume responsibility for cleansing it of vanity and hostility. As for Abū Ḥanīfa, who admitted the possibility of the abode of Islam returning to the abode of war, he made this conditional upon [1] the cessation of the observances (*shaʿāʾir*) of Islam and the establishment in their place of the laws of unbelief and [2] there not remaining any Muslim or *dhimmī* whose life is safe (a primary Islamic security) and [3] that it border the abode of unbelief or war. It is well-known that none of these three conditions is found in the occupied land. The observances of Islam remain public[ally practiced], Muslims enjoy the primary security and today there is no abode of unbelief or war bordering this land.

However, the shaykh [al-Albānī], who reckons himself as

8. Muḥammad Saʿid Ramaḍān al-Būṭī, *al-Jihād fī al-Islām: kayfa nafhamuhu? wa-kayfa numārisuhu?* (Beirut: Dār al-Fikr al-Muʿāṣir, 1997), 238-40.

"the *ḥadīth* transmitter of this age," has disregarded the *Sharīʿa*'s [doctrine of] consensus (*ijmāʿ*), of which he has no knowledge.[9] He then proclaimed to the people that Palestine has become, thanks to Israel, an abode of unbelief and war and, on account of this, it is obligatory for all of its Muslims to depart from it! The strange thing is that, all these long years, this suspect[10] shaykh has remained silent about having issued [this fatwā]. Not one of the chains of bitter events which have encircled this region and its people had reminded him about it. [It was not until] the light of the faithful Intifāḍa (Uprising) and the movement (Ḥamās) arose in the heart of this occupied land and, on account of this, an aura of terror spread to the hearts and souls of the occupiers, that the shaykh then remembered this ruling in which he had not formerly taken pride. He now saw fit to proclaim it in an explicit fatwā, published in all the media. Now that this intifāḍa has been launched, just when it has met with unexpected successes, he calls upon the leaders of this intifāḍa, and all the people of the truth and of the land, to abandon it. As though now they should give Israel relief from their string of disturbances and from the losses which have eroded their great riches.

It is truly obligatory for this suspect shaykh to inform us of the secret behind his reticence about this fatwā until today and about his silence regarding the sin of Muslims remaining in the abode of unbelief until this day! We truly thank God that this shaykh and his void fatwā were not present in the days when the Syrians, Algerians, Egyptians and Lebanese waged jihād in their homelands in order to cleanse them from the occupation of the colonizers and injustice of the tyrants. For if it had, it would have been obligatory for all of those

9. Al-Būṭī is accusing al-Albānī of having no knowledge of Islamic law despite possessing the deep knowledge of *ḥadīth* on which his reputation rests.

10. This term (*mashbūh*) was frequently used among Arab nationalists to indicate a collaborator with the imperialist powers and it is in this sense that al-Būṭī is using it. See Saʿad Jawad, *Iraq & the Kurdish question*, 1958-1970 (London: Ithaca, 1981), 104.

Muslims to depart from their lands which had become, according to his definition, an abode of war and the property of their enemies. We would look upon these [lands] today and see that those tyrants and colonizers had acquired them rightfully and lawfully. And who knows? Maybe this is what the shaykh likes and prefers.

In the new edition,[11] I now say, appending these lines to the [above] comment: We have been waiting for this shaykh to rescind his void fatwā – for returning to the truth is a virtue. However, he did not rescind it in spite of the Muslim world standing against him on account of it!

A minority of readers found my use of the word "the suspect" to describe the shaykh distressing. However, the meaning of this word is that a quasi-accusation of collaboration with a foreign region hovers around someone who issues a fatwā like this, and how many of them there are in this age. There is no doubt that a quasi-accusation is not an accusation in itself and is also not certainty of treason. Therefore, the word does not exceed the proper bounds, it is a strict description of a particular reality.

11. This text is from the second edition of the book which was published in 1997, the first edition was published in 1993.

SUGGESTIONS FOR FURTHER READING IN ENGLISH ON MUSLIMS UNDER NON-MUSLIM RULE

Primary Sources

Alwani, Taha Jabir. *Towards a Fiqh for Minorities: Some Basic Reflections*. London: International Institute of Islamic Thought, 2003.

Ibn Baz, ʿAbd al-ʿAziz ibn ʿAbd Allah and Muhammad ibn Saalih al-ʿUthaymeen, *Muslim Minorities—Fatawa Regarding Muslims Living as Minorities*. Hounslow: Message of Islam, 1998.

Qaradawi, Yusuf. *Fiqh of Muslim Minorities: Contentious Issues & Recommended Solutions* Cairo: Al-Falah Foundation for Translation, 2003.

Ramadan, Tariq. *Western Muslims and the Future of Islam*. Oxford: Oxford University Press, 2004.

Secondary Sources

Abou El Fadl, Khaled. "Islamic Law and Muslim Minorities: The Juristic Discourse on Muslim Minorities from the Second/Eighth to the Eleventh/Seventeenth Centuries." *Islamic Law and Society* 1 (1994): 141–187.

Caeiro, Alexandre. "Fiqh al-Aqalliyyat." In *Oxford Bibliographies Online: Islamic Studies*, accessed August 28, 2012, http://www.oxford-bibliographies.com/view/document/obo-9780195390155/obo-978019 5390155-0027.xml.

Haddad, Yvonne Yazbeck and John Esposito, eds. *Muslims on the Americanization Path?* New York: Oxford University Press, 2000.

Hardy, Peter. *The Muslims of British India*. London: Cambridge University Press, 1972.

Harvey, L. P. *Islamic Spain, 1250 to 1500*. Chicago: University of Chicago Press, 1990.

March, Andrew. *Islam and Liberal Citizenship: The Search for an Overlapping Consensus*. Oxford: Oxford University Press, 2009.

Peters, Rudolph. *Islam and Colonialism: The Doctrine of Jihad in Modern History*. The Hague: Mouton, 1979.

Robinson, David. *Paths of Accommodation: Muslim Societies and French*

Colonial Authorities in Senegal and Mauritania, 1880-1920. Athens: Ohio University Press, 2000.

Shadid, Wasef Abdelrahman and Pieter Sjoerd van Koningsveld. "Loyalty to a Non-Muslim Government: An Analysis of Islamic Normative Discussions and of the Views of Some Contemporary Islamicists." In *Political Participation and Identities of Muslims in Non-Muslim States*, ed. W. Shadid and P. van Koningsveld, 84-114. Kampen: Kok Pharos, 1996.

Umar, Muhammad S. *Islam and Colonialism: Intellectual Responses of Muslims of Northern Nigeria to British Colonial Rule*. Leiden: Brill, 2006.

OTHER TITLES IN THE PRINCETON SERIES OF MIDDLE EASTERN SOURCES IN TRANSLATION

General Editor, M. Şükrü Hanioğlu

Katip Celebi, *The History of the Maritime Wars of the Turks*. Expanded, edited, and annotated by Svatopluk Soucek. A newly edited and expanded edition—including newly translated texts—of this classic in naval history.

Heinz Halm, *The Arabs: A Short History*. Expanded edition with documents selected and edited by Luke Yarbrough and Oded Zinger. "A succinct account of Arab history packaged with an imaginative selection of lively and teachable primary sources."

—Michael Cook, Princeton University

Of Related Interest

African Slavery in the Mediterranean Lands of Islam edited and translated by John Hunwick and Eve Troutt Powell

Al-Jabartī's History of Egypt edited by Jane Hathaway

The Book of Strangers: Medieval Arabic Graffiti on the Theme of Nostalgia translated by Patricia Crone and Shmuel Moreh

Ibn Battuta in Black Africa edited and translated by Said Hamdun and Noel Q. King

Ibn Fadlan's Journey to Russia: A Tenth-Century Traveler from Baghdad to the Volga River edited and translated by Richard N. Frye

Jews of a Saharan Oasis by John Hunwick

Jihad in Classical and Modern Islam by Rudolph Peters

Memoirs of a Janissary by Konstantin Mihailović. Edited by Svatopluk Soucek and translated by Benjamin Stolz

Napoleon in Egypt: Al-Jabartī's Chronicle of the French Occupation, 1798 translated by Shmuel Moreh. Essays by Robert L. Tignor and Edward Said

Political Words and Ideas in Islam by Bernard Lewis

The Revolt of African Slaves in Iraq in the 3rd/9th Century by Alexandre Popovic

CPSIA information can be obtained at www.ICGtesting.com
Printed in the USA
BVOW05s1446010914

364840BV00001BA/16/P

9 781558 765726